REVIVAL OR WE DIE

REVIVAL OR WE DIE

A Great
Awakening is
Our Only Hope

MICHAEL L. BROWN PHD

DESTINY IMAGE® PUBLISHERS, INC.

P.O. Box 310, Shippensburg, PA 17257-0310

"Promoting Inspired Lives."

This book and all other Destiny Image and Destiny Image Fiction books are available at Christian bookstores and distributors worldwide.

Cover design by Eileen Rockwell

Interior design by Terry Clifton

For more information on foreign distributors, call 717-532-3040.

Reach us on the Internet: www.destinyimage.com.

ISBN 13 TP: 978-0-7684-5288-4

ISBN 13 eBook: 978-0-7684-5289-1

ISBN 13 HC: 978-0-7684-5291-4

ISBN 13 LP: 978-0-7684-5290-7

For Worldwide Distribution, Printed in the U.S.A.

1 2 3 4 5 6 7 8 / 25 24 23 22 21

CONTENTS

CHAPTER ONE

THERE IS MORE!

The words are simple and the sentence is short. Just three words total, eleven letters in all. *There...is...more.* That's it! And yet these three words articulate the cry of many a Christian's heart. Deep down, we know there is more.

It's not because we are malcontents or grumblers, or because we can never be satisfied. Instead, as we walk with the Lord, as we encounter His Spirit, as we look at Jesus, as we meditate on Scripture, as we look at the needs of the world, a cry rises to heaven from the depths of our heart: "Lord, there must be more!"

Speaking personally, God has not appointed me to be the judge of His Church. He has not called me to be a holy policeman or an accuser of the brethren. My goal is to build up, not tear down, and I thank God for everything He is doing in every church in the country, be it a house church or a mega-church. But I cannot deny that something is missing. I cannot deny that *there is more*. Does your own heart affirm these words as well? Then this book is for you.

Simply stated, if the Bible is true (which it is) and if Jesus really rose from the dead and sent the Spirit (which He did), then there must be more. There has to be more. Every page of the New Testament shouts to us that there is more. Why not be honest and say it out loud: "God, I know there must be more!"

To say that something is missing is to glorify the Lord. To say that something is not lining up is to be honest before heaven. To say that what you read in the Word is different from what you experience in life is to honor the testimony of Jesus.

He shed His blood so we could be transformed. So we could overcome the enemy. So we could be His Spirit-filled ambassadors. So we could set the captives free and heal the wounded and dying. There is so much more He still wants to do through you and through me.

He *longs* to manifest His grace in us and through us. He *longs* to reveal Himself to us. He *longs* to pour out His Spirit in power. He is more ready to bless and fill and ignite and anoint than we are to receive.

But are we ready? Are we hungry? Are we desperate? Do our prayers bleed? Do we have room for more of God's presence and power and purpose—in our hearts, in our homes, in our congregations?

Look carefully at the words of Jesus to the churches in Revelation.

To Sardis He said, "I know your deeds; you have a reputation of being alive, but you are dead" (Rev. 3:1). They looked good on the outside, but inwardly they were dead.

His words to Laodicea were even stronger: "You say, 'I am rich; I have acquired wealth and do not need a thing.' But you do not realize that you are wretched, pitiful, poor, blind and naked" (Rev. 3:17). They were the happening church, the prosperous church, the successful church—at least, in their own eyes—but in reality they were pitiful, poor, and blind.

There's a message here for us! When we are self-satisfied and proud, we will not be desperate for God. We will be filled with ourselves, with our programs and our meetings and our budgets and our activities and our self-congratulations. We have arrived! We have achieved our goals! Look at us!

There is no room for the Spirit's moving in a place like that, no room for visitation, no room for revival.

Like Laodicea, we boast of our wealth (be it spiritual or material); like Sardis, we think we are alive.

But God sees the condition of our souls, how we have exchanged the anointing for professionalism, how we have traded dependence on the Spirit for fleshly endeavors, how we have substituted a carnal business approach for our first love devotion. Now is the time to awaken!

What is the condition of *your* heart today? Are you hungry, thirsty, and desperate? If so, that is an excellent sign. Self-satisfaction is a spiritual curse. Be assured that there is more!

My Own Spiritual Journey

I got radically saved in 1971 as a heroin-shooting, LSD-using, 16-year-old, Jewish, hippie rock drummer. One year later, I was spending six or seven hours daily in prayer and the Word, including memorizing twenty verses a day, seven days a week. And how I loved to pray and worship and share my faith.

Eleven years later, while pursuing my Ph.D. in Near Eastern Languages and Literatures, I had become theologically proud and spiritually dry. I was still a committed believer. My wife and I took in Vietnamese refugees and helped other people in need, right in our own home. I still loved to teach and preach. But without a doubt, I had left my first love, and I needed to be revived.

Of course, I was the last one to recognize my own condition because the changes came gradually, and in some ways I *had* grown and matured. But others were praying for me, and by the end of 1982, I was a radically renewed man. The fire of God fell on me dramatically, and then, from me, it spread to many others in our congregation. We had been visited by the Holy Spirit in power. There was weeping. There was repentance. There was transformation. There was joy.

From that moment on, I knew that, more important than anything else in my life and ministry, I could not let the fire go out. I had to be a vessel of revival.

That became the consuming burden of my life—to see a sweeping, national revival—and in the spring of 1983, as I was gripped in intense intercession, I heard the Spirit say to me that I would be used in a revival that would touch the world.

My first reaction was to think, "You're crazy! You have gone off the deep end. You are deceived." But I could not deny the reality of that voice, a voice that kept speaking the more I fasted and prayed and cried out.

Thirteen years later, in the Spring of 1996, after writing books on revival and preaching around the world on revival and crying out to God for revival, the Lord called me to serve as a leader in the Brownsville Revival. There, in meeting after meeting for almost four straight years, the Lord reminded me of His promise: "Revival is real! You were right in believing for more!"

Saved at the Brownsville Revival

This testimony, written by Bryan Anthony, is typical of countless thousands of other testimonies we have heard and received over the years:

> In July of 1996, over a year into the revival, I was a 17-year-old atheist, regularly doing drugs, toting guns, given to drunkenness, filled with rage and bitterness, and battling suicidal thoughts.
>
> My great-grandfather was an AG [Assembly of God] pastor, a man of holy living, and an intercessor. I had been raised in the Assemblies, but at the age of 17, I had not yet been born from above.
>
> The youth pastor at my parents' church was planning a missions trip to a poverty stricken area in Medart, FL. His intentions were to stop for a day at the revival on the way down. My parents asked him if I could go along, and

his response was, "It's a missions trip. He's not even saved!" He agreed to pray about it, and the Lord impressed him to bring me along.

We arrived in Pensacola on July 20th, 1996, and showed up at Brownsville AG at about 1 p.m. Already, nearly a thousand people were gathered in a large bunch near the door, waiting for the meeting which began at 7 p.m.! As an unbeliever, I thought, "What is wrong with these people? They're nuts! Why are they so excited to get into an AG church?" I remember spontaneous hymns of praise rising from the throng while we waited outside in the hot Florida sun. "How Great Thou Art," "Amazing Grace," and several others. Passers-by on the street (the church met in the poorer area of the city) were hearing songs of praise to the Lamb of God, and this has been common in times of revival over the course of history. O, that every city would hear again of the glory of Christ, through the revived hearts of His people! But here I was, in the midst of the crowd, totally detached from their joy.

My hardened heart grew curious when the doors opened, as I saw men, women, and children moving quickly and earnestly for a seat in the building. As I walked into the building, even as a hardened sinner, I began to sense a difference in the atmosphere. A strange pull began to affect me. I felt increasingly uncomfortable about my sin, but there was an unspoken yearning for truth, reality, and salvation rising in my soul. I watched the people engaging in fervent and sincere worship and praise which lasted well over an hour, and a conviction of my sinfulness was intensifying. I attempted to put a wet blanket over it, even turning to the young man next to me and speaking in jest about the people worshipping around me. But I could not evade or circumvent the fact that something, or Someone, as real as He was invisible, was moving in the midst of this people.

The evangelist then brought up several women from South Korea, who had come to America to pray and street witness at the Atlanta Olympics. "What did you come to Brownsville for, dear sisters?" "To receive the Holy Spirit," they replied. Upon praying for them, they collapsed in a heap on the platform, with tears flowing copiously, crying out, "Oh God! Save souls in Atlanta.... Souls.... Souls...." The prayer went on for some time, and when it subsided, the evangelist began to preach. It was a passionate call to repentance, a cry to humble ourselves, turn from sin, have faith in the work of the cross, and receive the free mercy of Jesus Christ. I later discovered that this was his message every night at the Brownsville Revival, but on that night, I felt I was alone in a room with the preacher and the Holy Spirit.

The word was like a hammer that shatters the rock, and I could not resist the Spirit any longer. I understood clearly that I had to *"flee from the wrath to come"* and receive a new heart from the God of mercy. I was undone in my sin and overcome with the revelation of the cross of Christ. I was gloriously born from above that night, and nothing has been the same since. Glory to the Lamb that was slain!

When I went back to high school the next semester, 27 students called on the name of the Lord as a result of the transformation they saw in my life. I was immediately freed from the grip of drugs, alcohol, suicidal tendencies, and rebelliousness toward my teachers and parents. One day, I even jumped in my '89 Thunderbird and ran over more than 250 of my music CDs that were filled with immoral themes and profanity. What else could I do? I had experienced the cleanness of a forgiven heart for the first time, and I could not engage in that which contradicted it. I began preaching in youth gatherings, bearing witness to the Gospel on the streets, and leading prayer meetings.

In August of '97, I went back to Brownsville to attend the ministry school (at which Dr. Michael Brown was the President), from which I graduated in May of '99. It has been a remarkable journey with the Lord, and it all began on that day when I passed from the kingdom of darkness into the kingdom of His glorious Light. This was the experience of many thousands of souls who came to the Lord through the Brownsville Revival. We were witnesses of this for years, as we saw souls from every background—prostitutes, wealthy businessmen, thugs, and even preachers—bowed low before a holy God, crying out for mercy over their sin, having found that they were in need of cleansing as "God stepped down" in the midst of the gathering. Many souls, like myself, entered through the doors in unbelief, *"dead in trespasses and sins,"* and were born anew of the Spirit of God, saved to the uttermost by the power of the Gospel.

I remember many meetings when the fear of the Lord would grip the whole congregation of 4 or 5 thousand souls. Unbelievers were screeching and crying for mercy, intercessors weeping and wailing, and many throughout the crowd calling out, "Holy, holy, holy is the Lord...." Sometimes hours would go by in this manner, and you were gripped with the sense that brings to mind the words of an elder in the Hebrides revival:

"Tread lightly, for God Himself is hovering over us!"

I used to meet with a brother for prayer before our Bible school classes, and I recall pulling up to the school property in March of '98, where the student's morning prayer meeting was moved upon by the Lord in a profound way. When I pulled into the parking lot, students were prostrate all over the campus, laying in the grass or on the sidewalks, groaning with hunger for God, and asking Him for mercy on behalf of our nation. Strong men were broken before the Lord, trembling and weeping in prayer, and everywhere in these times the hearts of God's people seemed fixed on His throne. You were directed heavenward merely by being there. I felt as if I had stepped out of my car and into another world, where the earth was permeated with God Himself! O, that every community of saints would be marked with this kind of reality, for the glory of Christ![1]

What an amazing story—and again, I remind you, it was one of multiplied tens of thousands of equally dramatic, Jesus-exalting stories.

Yet there is *still more* that God wants to do. The Brownsville Revival, along with other recent outpourings and renewal movements, provides us with only a glimpse of everything the Lord has planned for His people. As Lee A. posted on my Facebook page, "The Brownsville revival has forever changed my life with feeling his power in a tangible way leaving me to always cry out, 'more Lord!'"[2] He will respond to that cry!

So say it out loud with me, slowly, clearly, and from your heart: *There...is...more.*

Notes

1. Bryan Anthony, "I Saw the Brownsville Revival," voice of Revolution, June 11, 2011 http://www .voiceofrevolution.com/2011/06/11/i-saw-the -brownsville-revival.

2. AskDrBrown, Facebook comment, November 15, 2020, https://www.facebook.com/AskDrBrown/posts/ 5360723183953240

CHAPTER TWO

REVIVAL OR WE DIE

John Knox prayed, "Give me Scotland or I die!" George Whitefield prayed, "Give me souls, or take my soul!" Today, tens of millions of Americans Christians need to pray, "God, give us revival or we die!"

There is no hyperbole in that prayer. Without a national awakening, America as we know it is doomed.

In 1944, Rev. Peter Marshall declared, "Surely the time has come, because the hour is late, when we must decide. And the choice before us is plain—Yahweh or Baal. Christ or chaos. Conviction or compromise. Discipline or disintegration."[1]

That was 1944, nine years before the first edition of *Playboy*. Compare that to the epidemic of internet porn today, affecting even our children. Marshall never could have imagined America falling this low. 1944 was a long time ago.

In 1959, Prof. Robert E. Coleman wrote:

> In a day when unprecedented numbers of people have a form of religion while at the same time the church seems unable to stem the rising tide of degeneracy that threatens the land, the question must be raised: Why this paradox? Should not the church have influence for righteousness in proportion to her numbers? However one may seek to answer this question, it is obvious that what we need is not more religion, but more power. In short, we need real revival![2]

And this was written *before* the counterculture revolution of the 1960s swept the nation. How much more urgently do "we need real revival" today?

In 1969 Dr. Bill Bright wrote, "We live in the most revolutionary period of human history.... Social band-aids and reform antiseptics give little hope for a cure or even an improvement. A revolution is needed.... You can experience this revolution. In fact, you can help bring it to pass."[3]

Also in 1969, Rev. Tom Skinner wrote, "I'm convinced America is at her crisis hour. *Revolution is inevitable.* It's just a matter of which faction is going to prove strongest and will win out in the end. I believe most Americans are so apathetic that they will just sit back and go to whoever wins the struggle."[4]

What would these men of God say today? 1969 was also a long time ago. It was the year of Woodstock. And it was the year of the Stonewall Riots.

But I doubt that the most zealous gay activist in 1969 would have predicted that the Supreme Court would one day redefine marriage. Or that the White House would light up in rainbow colors in celebration. Or that a "married" gay man would run for president. Or that another presidential candidate would say that transgender rights were the civil rights issue of our day. Or that a famous male athlete would be declared woman of the year. Or that the American Library Association would endorse drag queens reading to toddlers. No way!

And 1969 was four years before Roe v. Wade. Put another way, 1969 was four years before a court ruling would allow for more than 60 million babies to be aborted in their mother's wombs. How much more, then, do we need massive awakening today? How much more do we need a sweeping revival in the church that will spark a moral and cultural revolution in the society?

Where We Stand Today

Think about it for a moment. Even if Roe v. Wade was overturned, that would not change the hearts of tens of millions of Americans who would fight day and night for the "right" to abort. Even if we were able to push back against radical LGBT activism in the courts and the schools, that would not undo the damage that has been done. Nor would the LGBT community surrender any of the hard-earned victories they have won.

Back in the days of the sexual revolution of the late 1960s and early 1970s, which was also a time before the internet, no one could have imagined headlines like: "20 Mind-Blowing Stats About The Porn Industry And Its Underage Consumers."[5] Some of the stats cited include:

- 64% of young people, ages 13–24, actively seek out pornography weekly or more often.

- Porn sites receive more regular traffic than Netflix, Amazon, and Twitter combined *each month*.

- Recorded child sexual exploitation (known as "child porn") is one of the fastest-growing online businesses.

- 624,000-plus child porn traders have been discovered online in the U.S.

- The world's second-largest free porn site also received over 42,000,000,000 site visits during 2019 alone.

Who can even comprehend evil and abuse and perversion on this level?

Then there is the tragic breakdown of the family unit, with massive implications for the nation. As reported by the Brookings Review in 1996:

> In 1965, 24 percent of black infants and 3.1 percent of white infants were born to single mothers. By 1990 the rates had risen to 64 percent for black infants, 18 percent for whites. Every year about one million more children are born into fatherless families. If we have learned any policy lesson well over the past 25 years, it is that for children living in single-parent homes, the odds of living in poverty are great. The policy implications of the increase in out-of-wedlock births are staggering.[6]

Fast-forward to 2016, and the figures are even more staggering:

> In 2016, 28 percent of all births to non-Hispanic white women (i.e., white) occurred outside of marriage, a figure that is almost twice

as high as the 15 percent of births among this demographic that were nonmarital in 1990. In 2016, 52 percent of all births to Hispanic women occurred outside of marriage, up from 34 percent in 1990 (a more than 50 percent increase). The percent of births that occurred outside of marriage also increased for non-Hispanic black women (black) between 1990 and 2016, from 63 to 69 percent (a nine percent increase), though a much lesser extent than for white and Hispanic women.[7]

And when you factor in the effect of fatherlessness on the children, including dramatically higher likelihoods of crimes, delinquency, violent behavior, and promiscuity, you're talking about a mind-numbing national crisis.[8]

That's why there's only one real solution for the future of our country. We must have divine visitation. We must have revival. We must have awakening.

What else will turn the rising tide of opioid addictions? Or stop the vile sin of human trafficking? Or put broken families back together? Or heal the deep divisions that are tearing us apart?

In 1985, evangelical leader Carl F.H. Henry wrote:

Speaking for a national morality movement, an evangelical leader recently remarked: "The

United States has turned away from God. It mocks God. It worships a twentieth century Baal...incarnated in sensuality, material goods, and immorality of every kind..." Yet only a few years ago we were told that a new evangelical awakening had dawned in America; this very decade, it was said, is the decade of the evangelicals."[9]

That was more thirty-five years ago. And now, with the renewed rise of evangelical influence, which began with the 2016 election of Donald Trump, where we do find ourselves today? We are more hated, more reviled, and more marginalized than ever.

Witchcraft is on the rise. Radical feminism is on the rise. Marxism is on the rise. Transgender activism is on the rise. Mobocracy is on the rise. Abortion extremism is on the rise. Cancel culture is on the rise. We are in one of the darkest places that America has ever seen. Political victories alone cannot save the nation.[10]

Revival Can Turn the Tide

The good news is that American history has also been marked by great awakenings and revival movements, without which we would have crashed and burned a long time ago. The same thing can happen in our day.

To give one case in point, our nation was powerfully impacted by a prayer revival that swept the country in 1857-1858. Before that time, according to the revival scholar James Edwin Orr, the churches were becoming worldly and internalized, and immorality, violent crime, spiritualism, corruption, and atheism were on the rise. Does this have a familiar sound?

Jeremiah Lanphier, a retired businessman become missionary, acting in obedience to the Spirit's prompting, began to promote a weekly "Lunch Hour Prayer Meeting" for revival. Only six attended the first meeting, and twenty the second. But within several months, tens of thousands were praying seven days a week. The revival spread from city to city, jumped across the ocean to England, Ireland, and Wales, and shaped the history of our nation.

I have read that, from 1857-1858, over one million non-church members came to faith, in addition to one million formerly nominal church members. In fact, at the height of the revival there were reportedly more than *50,000 new births* a week.

As a result of this revival hitting Chicago, the forty-year ministry of D.L. Moody was born. And within a decade, slavery was legally abolished.

But there's more. As I noted in my 2017 book *Saving a Sick America*:

It is reported that in the early 1800's, Supreme Court Chief Justice John Marshall wrote to Bishop Madison of Virginia, "The church is too far gone ever to be redeemed." His observations were quickly swept away by the Second Great Awakening and seem shockingly ill-advised in retrospect. So much for the esteemed justice's foresight.

One century earlier, Rev. Samuel Blair, who became chaplain of the Congress of Pennsylvania, stated, "Religion lay as it were dying, and ready to expire its last breath of life in this part of the visible church..." This was shortly before the First Great Awakening, led by the great philosopher Jonathan Edwards, which radically impacted the society. "Religion" hardly expired and breathed its last breath.[11]

And these are only two striking examples out of several others that could be provided from our own national history.

The bottom line is this: No matter how dark things look, God can turn the tide. But we must get desperate. God will fill us in accordance with our hunger, but if we are filled with other things, we will have little room for Him. How hungry are we?

During my years in the Brownsville Revival, it was easy for us to believe for almost anything. After all, the testimonies we heard were so staggering, often impacting scores of young people within the same school. What if those sparks ignited into holy flames across the country?

These were the kinds of stories we heard day and night for years. Aletha R. wrote:

> I was 18 and asked to be a chaperone on a youth trip to a revival and was told we would go to the beach, too. All my 18-year-old ears heard was FREE BEACH TRIP so I agreed. To my dismay the first day they woke us up super early to get in line outside a church building...the sun wasn't even out yet and there were people in line already waiting for [the] evening service! We sat out there in the hot Florida sun for 12 hours before we were allowed inside—I wasn't the happiest but I knew whatever was happening had to be good. Worship was powerful and the message Steve Hill preached was intensely convicting. (I ran up to every single altar call that week!) By the end of the week I was getting baptized and declaring that I would never go back to my old ways. Up to that point I had been saved about

a year but still struggled to not be drawn to the world and my old ways. I got saved because I didn't want to go to hell, but I was constantly giving in to temptation. Lots of shame and guilt as well as fear that I wouldn't "make the long haul" as a believer.

After that week I was set on fire and hungered and thirsted for nothing but Him. The long drive home I wept cleansing tears the entire 12 hours—I couldn't even go inside the Cracker Barrel for the lunch break because I was in the back of the van being touched by His Spirit weeping. I didn't know my body could produce that many tears...some of the kids bought me Kleenex boxes and I used every single tissue before I got back home. Afterwards, there was a marked difference in me—holiness living was a byproduct but overall I was a woman unchained and liberated. No longer bound by my flesh and desire—completely set on fire for Him.[12]

Why can't God do this again today, except on a much larger scale? Is His arm shortened? Is His power reduced? Certainly not! And to ask again: What would happen if stories like this were multiplied by the millions across the nation? America would be shaken from coast to coast.

If the Spirit could touch Aletha and her friends like this more than twenty years (she is still on fire now), why couldn't He touch you and your friends today? And if He could do it for ten or twenty or a hundred or a thousand, why not for tens of millions?

Listen to Tom W.'s Brownsville Revival story. He, too, is still burning bright more than twenty years later:

> Before I knew them, my would-be youth pastor, his brother (a worship leader), and his father (who got saved at the 1970 Asbury Revival) were all involved with a Methodist church in Tulsa. They got a hold of Brownsville Revival tapes around 1996 and they were greatly impacted by God. They visited the revival and were massively touched by the Lord. They went home and started to become more radical in their capacities at the Methodist church, which led them to being essentially shown the door from the church.
>
> However, due to young people praying and worshiping at a birthday party they attended one Saturday night and God moving powerfully, they decided to meet again the following Saturday night. And again. And again. Eventually, they were meeting every Saturday

night and God brought along dozens and over several years, hundreds (if not thousands) of searching youth through the doors of rented buildings on Saturday nights. The group took dozens of trips down to Brownsville and each time many (like myself) were touched powerfully by the Lord.

One time (rather famously), the group was praying so much that they had to pull over their caravan of vans in Clarksville, Arkansas to a Citgo gas station, making quite the scene, with students laid out under the power of God on the ground at the gas station.[13] My youth pastor (Sam Mather) created the Revival Fire tape, which was copied and re-copied and went all around the world, touching unknown thousands.[14]

The ministry reached into the public schools and several high school youth groups (including mine) were led and influenced by those who had been to the revival. When I got saved in Fall '01, there was a definite move of God at my school, which was directly and indirectly impacted by the revival. I went to Brownsville (albeit on the tail end of the revival) in March '02 and I was greatly affected by the power of

God there and under the preaching of Steve Hill. The ministry lasts to this day and for those around my age that were touched by the ministry, the revival is a deep meaning shared experience that we will never forget. It ruined us.[15]

Can you imagine this happening in city after city and in county after county and in neighborhood after neighborhood and in family after family, with whole schools and churches touched by the power of God? It would be a national awakening.

The good news is that, without a doubt, God can do it again—and much, much more than we could ask for or imagine. The bad news is that the clock is ticking on our nation, as we are dangerously close to complete implosion.

So our prayer today is, "Do it again, Lord! Revive us or we die!" Do we have another choice?

Notes

1. Peter Marshall, "Trial by Fire: The Message of Elijah for Today," *Lamplighter* magazine, Lamb & Lion Ministries, March–April, 2007, 5–6.
2. Robert E. Coleman, "Introduction," in Henry C. James and Paul Rader, *Halls Aflame: An Account of the Spontaneous*

Revivals at Asbury College in 1950 and 1958 (Wilmore, KY: First Fruits Press, 2013), 13; accessed January 1, 2021, https://place .asburyseminary.edu/firstfruitsheritagematerial/66.

3. Bill Bright, *Revolution Now!* (Campus Crusade for Christ, 1969).

4. Tom Skinner, *Words of Revolution* (Grand Rapids, MI: Zondervan, 1970).

5. "20 Mind-Blowing Stats About the Porn Industry and Its Underage Consumers," December 4, 2020, https://fightthenewdrug.org/10-porn-stats-that -will-blow-your -mind.

6. George A. Akerlof and Janet L. Yellen, "An analysis of out-of-wedlock births in the United States," August 1, 1996, https://www.brookings.edu/research/an-analysis -of-out-of-wedlock-births -in-the-united-states.

7. Elizabeth Wildsmith, Jennifer Manlove, and Elizabeth Cook, "Dramatic increase in the proportion of births outside of marriage in the United States from 1990 to 2016," https://www.childtrends.org/publications/ dramatic-increase-in-percentage-of-births-outside -marriage-among-whites-hispanics-and-women-with -higher-education-levels.

8. See, for example, https://www.fatherhood.org/father -absence-statistic and https://fathers.com/statistics-and- research/the-consequences-of -fatherlessness/.

9. Carl F. H. Henry qtd. in Michael L. Brown, *It's Time to Rock the Boat* (Shippensburg, PA: Destiny Image, 1993), 40.

10. For an overview, see Michael L. Brown, *Jezebel's War with America: The Plot to Destroy Our Country and What We Can Do to Turn the Tide* (Lake Mary, FL: Frontline, 2019).

11. Michael L. Brown, *Saving a Sick America: A Prescription for Moral and Cultural Transformation* (Nashville, TN: Thomas Nelson, 2017), 183.

12. Aletha Rosemarie, Facebook comment, November 15, 2020, https://www.facebook.com/DrMichaelBrown/posts/10157515917425685.

13. "Appearance of the Holy Spirit," http://www.people.vcu.edu/~dbromley/brownsvilleholyspiritLink.htm.

14. Revival Fire Tulsa Ministries, "Revival Fire: side 1" (https://archive.org/details/RevivalFireSide1) and "Revival Fire: side 2" (https://archive.org/details/RevivalFireSide2). If you have never listened to this compilation, I strongly encourage you to do so.

15. Tom Watson, Facebook comment, November 15, 2020, https://www.facebook.com/DrMichaelBrown/posts/10157515917425685.

CHAPTER THREE

REDISCOVERING THE BOOK OF THE LAW

Josiah became king of Judah at the tender age of eight, and by the time he was sixteen he was diligently seeking the Lord. As Scripture records, "In the eighth year of his reign, while he was still young, he began to seek the God of his father David. In his twelfth year he began to purge Judah and Jerusalem of high places, Asherah poles and idols" (2 Chron. 34:3). He knew idolatry was wrong. He knew the people were in sin. And so, at the age of twenty, he was leading a national repentance movement.

Then, six years later, in the eighteenth year of his reign, something dramatic happened. The Temple itself had been compromised and corrupted for years. The very building that was supposed to be the holiest place on the earth had been filled with idol worship and per-verted sexual acts. The very Temple of the Lord had become a den of iniquity.

It was also in terrible disrepair, and so Josiah com-missioned the priests and Levites to clean up and restore the house of the Lord. What happened next changed the course of Josiah's life and the fate of the nation: "Hilkiah the high priest said to Shaphan the secretary, 'I have found the Book of the Law in the temple of the Lord.' He gave it to Shaphan, who read it. ...Then Shaphan the secretary informed the king, 'Hilkiah the priest has given me a book.' And Shaphan read from it in the pres-ence of the king" (2 Kings 22:8,10).

What? The Book of the Law, the Torah of Moses, had been lost for years? Worse still, the leaders didn't even realize it was missing? How could this be?

When Josiah heard the words of the Book, he was mortified, tearing his robes as a sign of mourning and holy outrage, then sending word to Huldah the prophet-ess to inquire about what was written. "Great is the Lord's anger," he said, "that burns against us because those who have gone before us have not obeyed the words of this book; they have not acted in accordance with all that is written there concerning us" (2 Kings 22:13).

Let's think about what happened here. Josiah had been leading a repentance movement for years, recognizing that his people were guilty of great sin in God's sight. But until the Word of God was rediscovered, he had no idea how bad things were or how angry God was. (As I have often said, we don't know what we don't know.) Then, in the midst of his repentance, he had an awakening. "Things are far worse than I imagined, and the Lord's wrath is about to be poured out!"

The prophet Huldah confirmed this, and so Josiah intensified his efforts to turn the heart of the nation. Wrath was about to fall.

> *Then the king called together all the elders of Judah and Jerusalem. He went up to the temple of the Lord with the people of Judah, the inhabitants of Jerusalem, the priests and the prophets—all the people from the least to the greatest. He read in their hearing all the words of the Book of the Covenant, which had been found in the temple of the Lord. The king stood by the pillar and renewed the covenant in the presence of the Lord—to follow the Lord and keep his commands, statutes and decrees with all his heart and all his soul, thus confirming the words of the covenant written in this book. Then all the people pledged themselves to the covenant* (2 Kings 23:1-3).

As a result, the repentance stepped into high gear. Read these words slowly, and then remember—this was taking place in the very house of the Lord. Yet with all the repentance and cleansing that had been going on, these obvious, horrific, despicable practices had still not been addressed—not until the Word was rediscovered.

> *The king ordered Hilkiah the high priest, the priests next in rank and the doorkeepers to remove from the temple of the Lord all the articles made for Baal and Asherah and all the starry hosts. He burned them outside Jerusalem in the fields of the Kidron Valley and took the ashes to Bethel. He did away with the idolatrous priests appointed by the kings of Judah to burn incense on the high places of the towns of Judah and on those around Jerusalem—those who burned incense to Baal, to the sun and moon, to the constellations and to all the starry hosts. He took the Asherah pole from the temple of the Lord to the Kidron Valley outside Jerusalem and burned it there. He ground it to powder and scattered the dust over the graves of the common people. He also tore down the quarters of the male shrine prostitutes that were in the temple of the Lord, the quarters where women did weaving for Asherah* (2 Kings 23:4-7).

To repeat—at this point, Josiah had been leading a repentance movement for years, even working on the cleansing and repairing of the Temple. And *still* all these abominations were being practiced. Compromise has a way of blinding our eyes, and we get used to the situation in which we find ourselves, comparing our own lives with the lives of others—until we rediscover the Word of God.

Laid Bare by the Holy Word

This is what happens to us when we experience true revival. Our eyes are opened, and we are undone. We are far more sinful than we realized. Far more worldly. Far more compromised. Far more polluted. Far more disobedient and dishonest and disloyal.

That also means that God is far more displeased with us than we understood. We thought we were so strong, so secure, so special. Now we realize we are hanging by a thread. The Word of God speaks to us afresh.

That's why Habakkuk cried out in that great revival verse, "In wrath remember mercy" (Hab. 3:2). That's why believers coming under acute conviction in times of true revival have cried out, "Hell is too good for me!" That's why, during great outpourings, pastors and Christian leaders feel as if they are getting saved all over again. True awakening will rock our world.

You might say, "But you can't compare us to Josiah's day because we haven't lost the Word. We read it and preach and teach out of it all the time."

To the extent that is true, then we are even more culpable. Sins committed with full knowledge are more serious than sins committed in ignorance.

Yet I question the idea that "we haven't lost the Word." How many born-again believers read the Word on a daily basis? How many have read the Bible cover to cover in the course of ten or twenty years? And how much of our preaching and teaching really gets us into the Word? No wonder that a recent survey indicated that biblical illiteracy in the Church worldwide has reached epidemic proportions.[1]

You might say, "In my church, we're hearing a steady dose of the Word. Our pastor uses the Bible in his sermons all the time."

I do hope that is true. But does he preach the whole counsel of God? (See Acts 20:25-27.) Does he preach on the holiness of God, one of the great themes of the entire Bible? Does he preach on our call to live holy lives, also one of the great themes of the Old and New Testament? Does he preach repentance, not merely as a change of mind but as a change of life? Does he call us to take up our cross, deny ourselves, and follow Jesus? Does he talk about the wrath of God, about the day of the Lord, about the coming judgment, and about the eternal consequences of sin?

You might say, "But you're mixing the covenants! We're not under wrath, we're under grace. And God's judgments were poured out on the cross. There will be no divine judgment in this age."

Well, you just proved my point. You really have lost the Word.

It is absolutely true that God has not appointed us for wrath but to obtain salvation (see 1 Thess. 5:9) and that we under grace, not law (see John 1:17; Rom. 6:14). But it is also absolutely true that God still judges here and now, during this age.[2]

The New Testament, from Jesus to Paul to Revelation, speaks frequently of the coming wrath, warning us not to partake in the deeds of the ungodly, because that wrath will fall on them.[3] As Revelation warns God's people living in Babylon, "'Come out of her, my people,' so that you will not share in her sins, so that you will not receive any of her plagues; for her sins are piled up to heaven, and God has remembered her crimes" (Rev. 18:4-5). This, too, is New Testament truth. It also explains why Jesus spoke far more about the fires of hell than the blessings of heaven. We need to be awakened.

You might say, "It's obvious you are a legalist with no concept of grace. God doesn't see our sins now. He sees us through the blood of the cross. Jesus took our judgment."

Actually, I love God's grace and walk in God's grace and preach God's grace day and night. We stand by mercy. We are empowered by love. We live by His faithfulness, not ours. And without a doubt, the Father always looks at us, His children, through eyes of compassion and kindness, and through the reality of the finished work of the cross.

The High Stakes of Grace

But that only means the stakes are higher. As it is written in Hebrews:

> If we deliberately keep on sinning after we have received the knowledge of the truth, no sacrifice for sins is left, but only a fearful expectation of judgment and of raging fire that will consume the enemies of God. Anyone who rejected the law of Moses died without mercy on the testimony of two or three witnesses. How much more severely do you think someone deserves to be punished who has trampled the Son of God underfoot, who has treated as an unholy thing the blood of

the covenant that sanctified them, and who has insulted the Spirit of grace? For we know him who said, "It is mine to avenge; I will repay," and again, "The Lord will judge his people." It is a dreadful thing to fall into the hands of the living God (Hebrews 10:26-31).

This is one of many passages I could cite from the New Testament with the very same message: the consequences of rejecting grace are much greater than the consequences of rejecting the Law.

Please read those verses from Hebrews again, and take special note of this question: "How much more severely do you think someone deserves to be punished who has trampled the Son of God underfoot, who has treated as an unholy thing the blood of the covenant that sanctified them, and who has insulted the Spirit of grace?" Do we take God's Word seriously or not?

As for the idea that God does not see our sin and that He only sees us through the cross, what do we do with Acts, with all the Letters, and with Revelation—in other words, with the rest of the New Testament after the Gospels? Virtually every one of these books addresses sin in the Church, often on page after page. If the Lord doesn't see our sins, why He is so grieved by them? Why the constant correction? We really need to rediscover the truth of the Word.

That's why, throughout the New Testament, we are warned about the danger of deception, either deceiving ourselves or being deceived by others.[4] As someone once said, the problem with deception is that it is very deceiving. Yet that is exactly what has happened to us in our day. We too have been deceived, and we don't even know it.

Look again at the words of Jesus to the churches of Sardis and Laodicea, which we quoted in the Chapter One, but this time, focusing on the power of self-deception. To Sardis, Jesus said, "These are the words of him who holds the seven spirits of God and the seven stars. I know your deeds; you have a reputation of being alive, but you are dead" (Rev. 3:1). Reputations can be deceiving. Very deceiving.

To Laodicea, Jesus said, "You say, 'I am rich; I have acquired wealth and do not need a thing.' But you do not realize that you are wretched, pitiful, poor, blind and naked" (Rev. 3:17). Appearances can be deceiving. Dangerously deceiving.

Really now, can you imagine being "wretched, pitiful, poor, blind and naked" and thinking that you are rich, wealthy, "and do not need a thing"? Can you imagine being that deceived? And yet many of us are, from pastors to ministry leaders to old believers and young believers. We have no clue how far we have fallen and how worldly we have become until we rediscover the Word.

Even in the midst of our sincere repentance, we often see things through our own eyes, failing to gain the perspective of the One "who has the sharp, double-edged sword," the One "whose eyes are like blazing fire and whose feet are like burnished bronze," the One who is "the faithful and true witness, the ruler of God's creation" (Rev. 2:12, 18; 3:14). When we rediscover His words, our eyes are opened and we are undone. Lord have mercy! Things are far worse than we realized.

This would be similar to a man experiencing back pain, thinking to himself, "I must have tweaked my back. I won't lift anything heavy for a few days." But when the pain only gets worse, he goes to the chiropractor who tries his normal adjustments. Yet nothing really works. "You better see your doctor," the chiropractor says.

So he goes to see his doctor, who says, "Let's take some x-rays," and then, a few days later, "Let's take some blood tests." Then the doctor sits him down and says, "I have bad news for you. This is very serious. You have cancer, and it has spread to your spine."

This is what happens when we rediscover God's Word—all of it. This is what happens when we come to the Lord in repentance knowing that something is wrong but having no idea just how wrong things are.

41

This is what happens when God looks at us with His x-ray vision. But He does it to save us, not destroy us. Our Lord reveals the sickness because He has the cure!

As He said to those same believers in Laodicea:

> *I counsel you to buy from me gold refined in the fire, so you can become rich; and white clothes to wear, so you can cover your shameful nakedness; and salve to put on your eyes, so you can see. Those whom I love I rebuke and discipline. So be earnest and repent. Here I am! I stand at the door and knock. If anyone hears my voice and opens the door, I will come in and eat with that person, and they with me. To the one who is victorious, I will give the right to sit with me on my throne, just as I was victorious and sat down with my Father on his throne. Whoever has ears, let them hear what the Spirit says to the churches* (Revelation 3:18-22).

Let us, then, fall to our knees with our Bibles open, reading God's words and being awakened to those words and coming to grips with the awful realities of our sin and disobedience. Let us also take hold of God's promises to pardon and restore, running to the throne of grace where we can obtain mercy and forgiveness (see Heb. 4:16). We are sicker than we realize but God's grace is nearer than we realize. Divine healing is our only hope, but we will never experience healing until we realize how sick we are. How we need the blood of Jesus!

Notes

1. See Leah MarieAnn Klett, "WEA head: Biblical illiteracy 'utmost problem' facing global evangelicalism, *Christian Post*, December 3, 2020, https://www.christianpost .com/news/wea-head-biblical-illiteracy-utmost-problem -facing-church.html?uid=07ed4df3d9. Among many other relevant articles focused on the American church, see Albert R. Mohler, "The Scandal of Biblical Illiteracy: It's Our Problem," January 20, 2016, https:// albertmohler.com/2016/01/20/the-scandal-of-biblical -illiteracy -its-our-problem-4; Ed Setzer, "The Epidemic of Bible Illiteracy in Our Churches," *Christianity Today*, July 6, 2015, https://www.christianitytoday.com/ edstetzer/2015/july/epidemic-of-bible-illiteracy-in-our -churches .html.

2. See Michael L. Brown, *Hyper-Grace: Exposing the Dangers of the Modern Grace Movement* (Lake Mary, FL: Charisma House, 2014), 149-166.

3. See, e.g., Luke 13:1-5; Ephesians 5:3-7; Colossians 3:5-6; Revelation 18:1-5.

4. Note in particular James 1:16-25; see also 2 Corinthians 11:2-4; Galatians 3:1.

CHAPTER FOUR

FROM AMAZING GRACE TO AMAZING SINNERS

Did you ever sing "Rock of Ages," the classic hymn written by Augustus Toplady (1740–1778)? The words ring true to this day:

> *Nothing in my hand I bring.*
> *Simply to thy cross I cling.*
> *Naked, come to thee for dress.*
> *Helpless, look to thee for grace.*
> *Foul, I to the fountain fly.*
> *Wash me, Savior, or I die.*

That's why the first words of the hymn are, "Rock of ages, cleft for me, let me hide myself in Thee." Outside of Him, there is no hope. Outside of Jesus, we are totally and utterly lost. That's why we come to the cross naked and helpless. That's why we *fly* to the fountain of God's grace. That why we cry out, "Wash me, Savior, or I die!"

It's either mercy or damnation, and the only one who can grant mercy is the righteous Judge who knows our every sin. And so Toplady wrote:

> *Not the labor of my hands*
> *Can fulfill Thy law's demands;*
> *Could my zeal no respite know,*
> *Could my tears forever flow,*
> *All could never sin erase,*
> *Thou must save, and save by grace.*

Have mercy on us, Lord God, and save us by Your grace. Otherwise, we perish. Otherwise, we are damned. Otherwise, it's all over, forever. This is Gospel 101.

That's why, when the Jewish crowd at Pentecost heard Peter's message, in which he told them they were guilty of crucifying Jesus the Messiah, "they were pierced to the heart and said to Peter and the rest of the apostles, 'Brothers, what should we do?'" (Acts 2:37 CSB) Or, as translated in the NET Bible, "they were acutely distressed."

The message hit home. The divine arrow pierced the heart. The conviction was intense. "Brothers, what shall we do? We are guilty of a terrible sin in God's sight. How can we make things right?"

And how did Peter respond? After calling on his fellow Jews to repent and be immersed in water, promising them forgiveness of sins and the gift of the Spirit in Jesus' name, Acts records, "With many other words he warned them; and he pleaded with them, 'Save yourselves from this corrupt generation'" (Acts 2:40).

He exhorted them. He urged them. He pleaded with them. He warned them. "Fly to the fountain of God's grace while you still have breath! Flee from the coming wrath! There is still time for mercy."

What a far cry all this is from today's feel-good gospel, the gospel of self-affirmation, the gospel of self-esteem, the gospel which is really no gospel at all. As explained on the 5 Minutes in Church History website, "Toplady knew that, apart from Christ, it's not that we simply won't become better people. We're not just 'okay people' apart from Christ. No, we're headed for the wrath of God over us, and unless Christ washes us with his precious blood and gives us his righteousness, we die. We die. That's what Toplady tells us in this hymn."[1]

That's why the best-known hymn of the twentieth century was "Amazing Grace," starting with those familiar words:

Amazing grace, how sweet the sound,
that saved a wretch like me.
I once was lost, but now am found,
was blind, but now I see.

The more clearly we see the depth of our sin, the more clearly we see the breadth of God's mercy. The more we realize the wretched nature of our rebellion, the more we understand the amazing nature of God's grace.

Yet today, we don't like to talk about coming to God as "wretches." That hurts our self-esteem! And rather than telling sinners how amazing the Lord's grace is, we tell them how amazing *they are*. No wonder there is so little conviction of sin today. No wonder there are so many shallow conversions—if they be conversions at all. No wonder there is so little depth in so much of the contemporary American Church.

Back to the Real Gospel

The bottom line is that if we are going to see true revival, then we will have to recover (or rediscover) the gospel. Conversely, one of the reasons we so desperately need revival is that we have strayed so far from the biblical gospel. In fact, we have turned the gospel upside down.

The biblical gospel proclaims that human beings are terribly sinful and that God's grace is truly amazing.

The American gospel proclaims that lost sinners are truly amazing and that any talk of God's judgment is really terrible. As for God's grace, it's like icing on the cake for the sinner—and be assured that the sinner's cake is already quite beautiful and wonderful. God just wants to add some special ingredients to make it taste even better.

"You're an amazing person and God is so into you! He has some really neat things to tell you about your future."

My friend, that is not the gospel, and sinners do not get saved by realizing how amazing they are. They get saved by realizing how lost they are and how amazing God's grace is, and that includes the message of His absolutely extraordinary love. But if the lost sinner is so amazing, why does he need to get saved? Why did Jesus even need to die for such an amazing person?

The biblical gospel declares that our sin is monstrous but that God sent His Son to take our place and suffer for our guilt. Today we are told that such a message turns God into a monster who practices cosmic child abuse.[2] So we have gone from recognizing that man is capable of doing monstrous things to claiming that the God who sent His Son to die in our place did something monstrous. How could this be?

As for the "neat things" that God wants to tell a sinner about his or her future, the inconvenient truth is that they include:

1. You are guilty in God's sight, and if you don't turn away from your sins and ask for mercy, you will perish.

2. One day you will stand before a holy, all-seeing, all-knowing Judge, one who doesn't take bribes and who doesn't care about public opinion. On that day, all your excuses will vanish in His sight.

3. If you refuse His grace and scorn His goodness, saying to Him in this life, "I don't want anything to do with you. Get away from me!" then in the world to come, He will say those words back to you: "I don't want anything to do with you. Get away from Me—forever!"

4. If you acknowledge your guilt today, ask Him for mercy, believe that Jesus died for your sins and rose from the dead, and confess Him as Lord, He will wash away every sin, cleanse you from the inside, give you eternal life, fill you with His Spirit, make you His child, change your heart

and desires, enlist you in His service, and spend eternity with you in unimaginable bliss, satisfaction, and joy.

Now we're preaching the gospel.

The fact of the matter is that true repentance always goes deeper than we expect, both for the sinner and for the saint. That's why it's so uncomfortable. That's why so many resist it. That's also why it is so necessary. We are sicker than we realize and the cure is more radical than we imagine. God can truly change us!

Remember, Jesus did not come to improve us or enhance us or make us bigger and better or more successful. He came to save us from our sins, to forgive us and transform us, to transfer us from death to life and from the kingdom of satan to the kingdom of God. That's the gospel. He came so we could die to our old rebellious ways and live new lives of obedience in Him.

Sadly, this has been one of the greatest problems in America for several decades now—shallow preaching producing shallow converts, or, even worse, counterfeit preaching producing counterfeit converts. Adding insult to injury, these shallow (or counterfeit) converts don't have any idea that they are shallow (or counterfeit), because this is the "gospel" they were exposed to. And to make matters worse still, the shallow and counterfeit messages inoculate them to the true message when they do hear it. "That's legalism!" they cry. "You're not going to put any condemnation on me!" And so, they miss the true message of life because they have been sold a bill of shoddy (or counterfeit) goods.

True Revival and the True Gospel Go Hand in Hand

In my 1993 book, *It's Time to Rock the Boat: A Call to God's People to Rise Up and Preach a Confrontational Gospel*, I cited some examples of how the true gospel message, preached with the anointing of the Spirit, pierces hearts and lives. From the soul-saving ministry of William Booth (1829–1912) comes this eyewitness account of a truly evangelistic service: "Penitent sinners have come up the aisle so overcome as to be hardly able to reach the rail. Fathers and sons, mothers and daughters have knelt side by side weeping. [Remember, these were *lost sinners* coming forward to be saved.] ...The preacher was again earnest, *terrible*, melting, full of pathos. The Word was with power."

William Booth's wife Catherine (1829–1890) describes another evening outreach: "The communion rail was filled in a few minutes with great strong men who cried aloud for mercy, many as though the pains of hell had actually got hold of them. The cries and the shouts of the penitents almost overpowered the singing. At night there was a gale of saving grace....The meeting did not finally close until 3 a.m. and the chapel was open the next day."

Or consider the great outpouring that occurred July 23, 1839 at Kilsyth, Scotland, during the preaching of William C. Burns. Under an overwhelming unction from on high, he pleaded with the unconverted to receive God's mercy at that very moment and, he says:

> I continued to do so until the power of the Lord's Spirit became so mighty upon their soul as to carry all before it, like the "rushing mighty wind" of Pentecost.
>
> They broke forth simultaneously in weeping and wailing, tears and groans, intermingled with shouts of joy and praise from some of the people of God. The appearance of a great part of the people from the pulpit gave me an awfully vivid picture of the state of the ungodly in Christ's coming to judgment. Some were screaming out in agony; others— and among these, strong men—fell to the ground as if they had been dead. This was the morning service, which, however, went on

until three in the afternoon, and was only dismissed on the announcement of a resumption at six o'clock; and such was the general commotion that, after repeating the most free and urgent invitation of the Lord to sinners (as Isa. 55:1 and Rev. 22:17). I was obliged to give out a Psalm, which was soon joined in by a considerable number, our voices mingled with the mourning groans *of many prisoners sighing for deliverance.*[3]

On a regular basis, we saw scenes like this in the Brownsville Revival, as lost sinners and backslidden believers would literally run to the altar to get right with God. Even leading pastors would rush forward and fall to their knees in repentance, telling us afterward, "I brought my people here because they needed a fresh touch from God. It turns out I was the one who needed that fresh touch more than any of them! I feel like I got born again all over again." And if that is what happened to pastors and believers, you can only imagine what happened to those who didn't know the Lord at all.

During the revival, we did not allow visitors to take pictures or record videos during the services, but we did have a church photographer and all the services were professionally videotaped. Then, on special occasions when a major media outlet was doing a story on the revival, we would allow their camera crew to film the service. And sometimes, when a news outlet like the *New York Times* would cover the revival, they would send a photographer to take pictures all night, looking for just the right shot to use for their story.[4]

One night, a professional photographer came to take pictures for the cover story of his publication. I don't recall which publication he was working for, but I do recall that he took pictures non-stop through the service. And because it was in the days before digital photography, he was constantly changing the rolls of film. From my vantage point sitting on the platform with the other leaders, it was hard to miss him, as he moved from place to place to get the best angles and as he shot away during our extended time of worship.

Steve Hill then preached his typical, in-your-face repentance message, and I'm sure the photographer took pictures of his preaching too. After all, he was there to do a job, not listen to a sermon. But he must have been listening too, and when Steve gave the altar call, this photographer was one of the first ones to respond. It was quite a sight to see!

When he reached the altar, he fell to his knees sobbing, with the camera around his neck, just a few feet away from me. He was overcome by the conviction of the

Spirit. Then, realizing he had an amazing photo opportunity, he managed to stop convulsing for a moment, look over at the others weeping at the altar, take a few more pictures, then continue to weep and repent. This cycle repeated itself several times. That is the power of the gospel.

In my 1995 book *From Holy Laughter to Holy Fire: America on the Edge of Revival*, which was released three months before the Brownsville Revival began, I devoted one chapter to the subject of conviction. Some of the powerful quotes cited in that chapter included this, from Duncan Campbell, describing scenes from the Hebrides Revival in 1949:

> [Another] main feature [of the 1949 Hebrides revival] has been deep conviction of sin—at times leading almost to despair. I have known occasions when it was necessary to stop preaching because of the distress manifested by the anxious, and many would find expression for the feeling in their hearts and the burden of their guilty conscience, in the words of John Newton:
>
> "My conscience felt and owned its guilt,
> And plunged me in despair;
> I saw my sins His blood had spilt

And helped to nail Him there."

[In the parish of Uig] all lorries and vans available were put into service to convey the people to the place of worship, yet many were forced to walk miles; but distance did not matter, and at any rate they knew that the meetings would continue: if they were not in time for the first, they would be sure of getting the second or the third. So they came across the moors and over the hills, young men and maidens, their torches flashing in the darkness, intent upon one thing, to get peace from a guilty conscience, and refuge from the storm in their bosom, in the shelter of the Rock of Ages.[5]

For good reason W. Graham Scroggie said, "There has never been a spiritual revival which did not begin with an acute sense of sin."[6] When the holy God begins to speak and act in the midst of a compromised church and a rebellious world, it is inevitable that conviction will come. How can it not?

That's why Charles Spurgeon said:

A spiritual experience which is thoroughly flavored with a deep and bitter sense of sin is of great value to him that hath it. It is terrible in the drinking, but it is most wholesome in the bowels, and in the whole of the afterlife.

Possibly, much of the flimsy piety of the present day arises from the ease with which men attain to peace and joy in these evangelistic days. We would not judge modern converts, but we certainly prefer that form of spiritual exercise which leads the soul by the way of Weeping-cross, and makes it see its blackness before assuring it that it is "clean every whit."

Too many think lightly of sin, and therefore think lightly of the Savior. He who has stood before His God, convicted and condemned, and with the rope about his neck, is the man to weep for joy when he is pardoned, to hate the evil which has been forgiven him, and to live to the honour of the Redeemer by whose blood he has been cleansed.[7]

Not that long ago, I read an Instagram post by a very famous performer who is not ashamed to speak about his Christian faith. In the post, he was thanking God for forgiveness, grateful that, in Jesus, his shame had been removed. And I do appreciate the message he was sharing: There is mercy and grace for the worst of sinners. That's why Jesus died for us.

But there was something else in the post that put forth a mixed message. This celebrity explained that Jesus was "honored" to know everything about our lives, both the good and the bad. And he assured his millions of followers that Jesus wasn't angry with them, only wanting what was best for them.

To be sure, Jesus does want what is best for us. I affirm that will all my heart. But to say that the Lord of heaven and earth is "honored" to know about our sins is to turn the gospel upside down. Jesus is "honored" to know about the worst things we've ever done? Really? Why on earth would He be "honored" to know about our sexual sins, our violent deeds, our ugly thoughts, our hurtful acts, our perverse desires? Grieved, yes. Honored, no.

We might as well give altar calls like this: "Jesus considers it an honor that you've come to the meeting tonight, and He counts it a privilege to know about your dirty secrets. He would be so blown away if you would ask Him into your life tonight." That is not the gospel.

As I wrote in *How Saved Are We?*:

> Yet we apologetically try to present the gospel
> to our hearers as if they would be doing Jesus
> a favor by receiving Him into their hearts. We
> tell them, "It's OK. Don't worry about change.

You really don't have to forsake anything. Just ask Jesus to come in!" But He is the Lord of all, and He says, "You come to Me!" He is the pearl of great price. We are indebted to Him.

"The trouble is the whole 'Accept Christ' attitude is likely to be wrong. It shows Christ applying to us rather than us to Him. It makes Him stand hat-in-hand awaiting our verdict on Him, instead of our kneeling with troubled hearts awaiting His verdict on us. It may even permit us to accept Christ by an impulse of mind or emotions, painlessly, at no loss to our ego and no inconvenience to our usual way of life" (A. W. Tozer). But Jesus and the old life don't mix. We are called to press upward to Him.

How would a young man feel after he proposed to the woman he loved if she looked at him and said: "Yes, I'll marry you. But do I have to give up my other boyfriends? Will you want me back home every night? Can I still sleep around and have fun?" What would his reaction be? He would be hurt and disappointed. He would be deeply shattered and shocked. He expected her unswerving loyalty. He wanted a true mate for life.

What about Jesus our heavenly Bridegroom? Does He deserve less than that? Will He accept sinners if they do not pledge Him their loyalty? Yet we are afraid to tell the unregenerate that they must give up their "other lovers" if they want to be joined to Him. We don't want to turn them off! What a pitiful mentality.[8]

But *How Saved Are We?* came out in 1990, since which time our gospel standards have fallen even further, helping to produce the current spiritual crisis in which we find ourselves today. The good news is that the true gospel still packs the full power of God to deeply transform lives. We must return to it before it's too late. The last thing America needs is a half-baked, superficial, pseudo-gospel—a "gospel" that is really not the gospel at all, because it doesn't save or deliver or transform.

America is sin-sick to the point of death. We don't need a pretty Band-Aid. "For the wages of sin is death, but the gift of God is eternal life in Christ Jesus our Lord" (Rom. 6:23). Let's preach this as if the fate of the nation depended on it—because, in fact, it does.

Notes

1. "Augustus Toplady," FEBRUARY 19, 2020, https://www.5minutesinchurchhistory.com/augustus -toplady.

2. For my relevant debate with Pastor Brian Zahnd, see https://www.youtube.com/watch?v=T27av -RF2-Y.

3. Quoted in Brown, *It's Time to Rock the Boat*, 78-80, emphasis in the original.

4. For the record, the *Times* posted a very positive story that, for some reason, made it to the front page of the main section of the paper (not the Religion section), and at that time, the *Times* was much more influential than it is today. According to the story, the Brownsville Revival was "apparently the largest and longest-running... revival in America in almost a century." See https://www.encyclopedia.com/religion/legal-and-political -magazines/brownsville-revival.

5. Michael L. Brown, *From Holy Laughter to Holy Fire: America on the Edge of Revival* (expanded, second edition; Shippensburg, PA: Destiny Image, 1996), 93-94.

6. Quoted in Brown, *From Holy Laughter to Holy Fire*, 90.

7. Quoted in Brown, *From Holy Laughter to Holy Fire*, 102-103.

8. Michael L. Brown, *How Saved Are We?* (Shippensburg, PA: Destiny Image, 1990), 16-17.

CHAPTER FIVE

A PSALM OF REPENTANCE

It is true that the true gospel calls lost sinners to repentance. But that same gospel calls believers to repentance as well, especially during times of revival. In fact, the repentance normally begins with us, the saved, before going out to the backslidden and the lost, as we become deeply aware of our own sin in light of the fresh visitation of God's holiness.

But the Lord not only calls us to repent. Through His Word, and through His people in Scripture, He models true repentance for us. There is no better example than Psalm 51.

The superscription reads: "For the director of music. A psalm of David. When the prophet Nathan came to him after David had committed adultery with Bathsheba." But the Hebrew is actually more vivid, using the words "come to" twice: Nathan came to David after David came to Bathsheba. As rendered in the NASB, David wrote the psalm "when Nathan the prophet *came to him*, after he had *gone in to* Bathsheba" (my emphasis).

The adulterous visit of the king produced a righteous visit from the prophet, reminding us that sin often has direct and corollary consequences. And it was the rebuke of Nathan that struck the heart of David, after which he wrote Psalm 51. But before we examine the depth of David's repentance, we need to understand how deeply he betrayed the Lord.

We read in Second Samuel 11 that, at the times when kings went out to war, David stayed back in Jerusalem. This was out of character for the warring king, and it points to a lack of sharpness in his life. The king of Israel was not being vigilant.

From the roof of his palace, he noticed a beautiful woman bathing on her rooftop. Immediately, he sent his people to find out who she was, and they informed him that she was married to Uriah the Hittite. But that didn't stop David from sending for her at once. He was the king, after all, and if he wanted to have sex with a married woman, that was his prerogative. Power and a sense of divine favor can be very intoxicating.

How many anointed Christian leaders have tarnished or even destroyed their ministries by playing games with sexual sins? "I'm anointed," they reason to themselves, "and the favor of God is on my life. I'm privileged." Soon enough, they are acting like brute animals, throwing aside their sacred callings and shaming their own families in order to fulfill their physical and emotional lusts.

Take heed, my brother and my sister. If we are not careful, the same thing could happen to any of us. And be assured—if you play with fire long enough, you will get burned.

David's World Spins Out of Control

Not long after their sexual encounter, Bathsheba sent word to David: "I'm pregnant." Things just went from bad to worse. Now David went into cover-up mode.

He pulled Uriah out of battle—he was out fighting where David should have been—called him into the palace, asked how the battle was going, and sent him home. "Surely," David thought, "Uriah has been away for many days and will sleep with his wife tonight. Then, he'll just think the baby was his, even if it's early." But Uriah had so much honor that, rather than go home to Bathsheba, he slept outside the palace with the other troops.

So David took things one step further. He invited Uriah back to the palace for a second day, got him drunk, and then sent him home. But even while drunk, Uriah would not go home, sleeping outside the palace again. At that moment in time, even a drunk Uriah had more integrity than a sober David. That is how sin degrades our whole character.

What, then, was David to do? He sent a note to his general, Joab, telling him to put Uriah on the front lines of the battle, then to draw back from him, leaving him to be killed. In other words, David ordered Uriah to be murdered. From lust, to adultery, to lies, to murder. This is the descent of sin. And note this—David sent the instructions to Joab *through Uriah himself.* This faithful man, Uriah, carried his own death sentence with him and delivered it to the man who would orchestrate his killing. David knew that Uriah could be trusted.

Even when Joab sent word to David that Uriah had been killed, the king showed no remorse, sending word back to Joab, "'Do not be distressed about the matter. The sword always takes its toll. Press your attack on the city and destroy it!' Encourage him!" (2 Sam. 11:25, NJPS). These things happen! Don't let it trouble you.

Now, with Uriah out of the way, after giving Bathsheba time to mourn, David took her as his wife. His sin was hidden. Uriah was gone. David could move on with his life.

Except he couldn't. God had been watching every single moment. Watching David as he stayed behind and was derelict in his duty. Watching as David cast his eyes on Bathsheba. Watching as he hardened his heart upon learning that she was married. Watching as he called her into the palace for sex. Watching as he got word about the pregnancy. Watching as he tried to coax Uriah into thinking the child was his own. Watching as he gave instructions to Joab to have Uriah killed. Watching as he received the word of this faithful man's murder. Watching as he took Bathsheba as his wife. Could he really think a holy God would simply let him slide?

David, after all, was entrusted with the kingship of God's own people, taken as a shepherd boy and put into the royal palace. The Lord had specially gifted him to write beautiful songs and prayers, the very psalms we recite three thousand years later. He had become one of the most powerful men on the planet, a man whose name would one day occur in the Bible more than any person outside of Jesus Himself. And he had multiple wives and concubines. Why did he have to take a loyal soldier's one and only wife?

The reality is that David must have been in a compromised state from the start. Otherwise, he would never have sent for Bathsheba in the first place. Or, if somehow he yielded to overwhelming temptation (after all, with the snap of his fingers, he could make his wishes come true), if his heart had been tender, he would have repented deeply at once. He would have asked Bath-sheba's forgiveness. He would have confessed to Uriah. Instead, his heart only grew harder—until Nathan the prophet was sent to him.

Perhaps this is where you find yourself today. You have left your first love, becoming complacent and com-promised. The things that used to convict you no longer do. Your prayer life is practically non-existent. You have not encountered God in worship in months (or years). As for ministry work, you stopped leaning on the Lord a long time ago, learning how to perform and put on a show. And the sins you have been committing behind the scenes have become more frequent, more risky, more vile, leading to a deepening sense of guilt and a grow-ing self-deception. And then the prophet comes with a word from the Lord and you are smitten. The Spirit pierces your heart and the love of God confronts your soul. Now you are undone. How do you respond?

"You Are the Man!"

Let's go back to David's story, which is recounted in Second Samuel 11–12. Chapter 11 ends with this verse: "After the time of mourning was over, David had

[Bathsheba] brought to his house, and she became his wife and bore him a son. But the thing David had done displeased the Lord" (2 Sam. 11:27). God was about to speak:

The Lord sent Nathan to David. When he came to him, he said, "There were two men in a certain town, one rich and the other poor. The rich man had a very large number of sheep and cattle, but the poor man had nothing except one little ewe lamb he had bought. He raised it, and it grew up with him and his children. It shared his food, drank from his cup and even slept in his arms. It was like a daughter to him.

"Now a traveler came to the rich man, but the rich man refrained from taking one of his own sheep or cattle to prepare a meal for the traveler who had come to him. Instead, he took the ewe lamb that belonged to the poor man and prepared it for the one who had come to him."

David burned with anger against the man and said to Nathan, "As surely as the Lord lives, the man who did this must die! He must pay for that lamb four times over, because he did such a thing and had no pity."

Then Nathan said to David, "You are the man! This is what the Lord, the God of Israel, says: 'I anointed you king over Israel, and I delivered you from the hand of Saul. I gave your master's house to you, and your master's wives into your arms. I gave you all Israel and Judah. And if all this had been too little, I would have given you even more. Why did you despise the word of the Lord by doing what is evil in his eyes? You struck down Uriah the Hittite with the sword and took his wife to be your own. You killed him with the sword of the Ammonites. Now, therefore, the sword will never depart from your house, because you despised me and took the wife of Uriah the Hittite to be your own.'

"This is what the Lord says: 'Out of your own household I am going to bring calamity on you. Before your very eyes I will take your wives and give them to one who is close to you, and he will sleep with your wives in broad daylight. You did it in secret, but I will do this thing in broad daylight before all Israel.'"

Then David said to Nathan, "I have sinned against the Lord."

Nathan replied, "The Lord has taken away your sin. You are not going to die. But because by doing

this you have shown utter contempt for the Lord,
the son born to you will die" (2 Samuel 12:1-14).

The divine arrows pierced David's heart—"You are the man!"—and he repented on the spot. "I have sinned against the Lord," David said. No excuses, no justification, no evasion. Just a clear acknowledgment of guilt.

A Heartfelt Plea for Mercy and Cleansing

But that was not the only thing he said. Subsequent to Nathan's visit, David wrote Psalm 51. These are the opening words:

> *Have mercy on me, O God, according to your unfailing love; according to your great compassion blot out my transgressions. Wash away all my iniquity and cleanse me from my sin* (Psalm 51:1-2).

Sin defiles us, dirties us, damages us, destroys us. Sin stains us—deeply. And when the Spirit convicts us of our sins, we know how guilty we are, how much we deserve judgment and damnation, how our only plea is for mercy. Yet the mercy we need is great and vast, greater than any human being can supply. We need mercy in keeping with the greatness of God's unfailing love (in Hebrew *chesed*, which speaks of His covenant kindness), in accordance with His abundant compassion. Without that, there is no hope. Without that, it is over. Without that, we are doomed.

Picture it like this. You're a married man, like David, but you say to yourself, "I've never slept with another woman, let alone killed someone, like he did. I'm really a pretty good guy. Maybe I glance at some videos on the internet, and yes, I've had my share of unclean thoughts. But I've never done what David did."

And then you stand before the Judge, who has a complete record of all those internet videos you've watched. A few here, a few there, a day here, a night there, and before you know it, there are thousands of porn clips you have viewed. How many thousands of unclean acts have you witnessed? As for the lustful thoughts—thoughts where you undressed another man's wife and had sex with her—those now come up on your record, also adding up to the thousands, every one of them adulterous. Suddenly, you can relate to David's words in another psalm: "my sins have overtaken me, and I cannot see. They are more than the hairs of my head" (Ps. 40:12). "I am guilty in Your sight, O God!"

How wonderful it is that our perfect, all-knowing, righteous Lord is also a merciful and compassionate Father. The same eyes that are too holy to look on sin, the same eyes that convict us of our guilt, are the same eyes that look with tenderness toward us when we humble ourselves and repent.

But in Psalm 51, David knows how deeply corrupt he has become, and he wants his sins blotted out. He wants them forgiven and forgotten, removed from the book of reckoning. Not only so, but he wants to be washed and cleansed—thoroughly. The stench of his filth is all over him. Only God's mercy, expressed most fully through the blood of Jesus, can make him clean again.

Have you ever experienced this in your own life? Have you ever felt that dirty, that ugly, that soiled? I remember back to 1971, shortly before I came to faith. I had been a proud sinner, boasting about my transgressions. Then, people I barely knew (if at all) began to pray for me, although I had no idea they were praying, and soon enough the Spirit was convicting me of my guilt.

I vividly remember lying in bed at night high on drugs, feeling absolutely miserable about my ungodly behavior. But just one week before, also high on drugs, lying in that same bed, I thought about my sinful escapades with delight. "Am I cool or what?" Now, thinking about those very same things, I was ashamed and smitten. It felt as if something was under my skin, eating away at me, but I didn't know how to get rid of it.

Thankfully, the night I surrendered to the Lord, telling Him I would never put a needle in my arm again, all the guilt was gone. All of it! The worst memory I could think of couldn't conjure up any guilt at all. The blood of Jesus had blotted out my sins! I stood clean before my Lord!

Since then, as a follower of Jesus, at key times the Holy Spirit has convicted me of disobedience or compromise in my life, sometimes very deeply. (If you've never experienced the Spirit's piercing love as a believer, uncovering sin in order to draw you closer to the Lord, I question the depth of your intimacy with God.) On one occasion, I remember the conviction getting so intense that I wanted to crawl out of my skin as I lay on my face pounding the floor and crying out. But, as penetrating as the divine conviction was, the outpouring of mercy was even greater, and as painful as the purging was, the new growth and life that came out of it was absolutely worth it.

Tragically, in our day, there is a dangerous doctrine that claims that the Holy Spirit no longer convicts believers of sin. It claims that the Holy Spirit only convicts the world of sin, not the believer, based on a misinterpretation of John 16:7-11. I took time to demolish that false teaching in the book *Hyper-Grace*, which I encourage you to read if you have been led astray by this lie.[1]

Thank God that the Spirit convicts us (not condemns us). Thank God that He doesn't allow us to get comfortable in our sin. Thank God that He reveals our sickly spiritual condition, not to push us away but to draw us near. He convicts us because He loves us. As Jesus said in Revelation 3:19, "Those whom I love I rebuke and discipline. So be earnest and repent." (Note that the Greek word translated "discipline" here is the same word translated "convict" in John 16:8.)

So, in the words of Psalm 95, repeated in Hebrews 3, "Today, if you hear His voice, do not harden your heart." Pray as David prayed: "Have mercy on me, God, according to your incredible love and faithfulness. Blot out all my sins. Wash me clean!"

He continued:

> *For I know my transgressions, and my sin is always before me. Against you, you only, have I sinned and done what is evil in your sight; so you are right in your verdict and justified when you judge. Surely I was sinful at birth, sinful from the time my mother conceived me. Yet you desired faithfulness even in the womb; you taught me wisdom in that secret place. Cleanse me with hyssop, and I will be clean; wash me, and I will be whiter than snow* (Psalm 51:3-7).

David did not deny a thing. His sin was there, right in front of his eyes, just as it had been for weeks before.

He tried to get on with his life, but his sin remained. Yet there was more that he understood as he wrote this psalm.

It was true that he sinned in the vilest way against Uriah, first having sex with his wife, then trying to deceive him, then killing him. What could be worse than that? He had also sinned against Bathsheba, however willing she might have been. After all, he was the king. And he had sinned against his trusted confidants, not to mention his other wives, not to mention the nation that depended on him.

But at that moment, under the glaring spotlight of the Spirit, he knew one thing: He had sinned against God. He was guilty in the sight of the Judge. The one to whom he had to give ultimate account was the one he had despised and disdained. "I have sinned against You alone!"

This is an important principle we must grasp, even as we work to rebuild the trust of those we have sinned against here on earth and even as we pursue reconciliation. *All sin is first and foremost sin against God.*

And because we know our own guilt, we know that God is perfectly righteous in what He does. In other words, the world might think we are being treated unfairly, but we know the depth of our wrong deeds. God is perfectly just when He judges.

Yet David's confession goes deeper still. He recognizes that he was born with a sinful nature,[2] which is why the cleansing must go deeper as well. "Lord, don't just cleanse me on the outside. I need to be scrubbed on the inside as well! And when you do the cleaning, I will be clean—white as snow."

He continued:

> *Let me hear joy and gladness; let the bones you have crushed rejoice. Hide your face from my sins and blot out all my iniquity. Create in me a pure heart, O God, and renew a steadfast spirit within me. Do not cast me from your presence or take your Holy Spirit from me. Restore to me the joy of your salvation and grant me a willing spirit, to sustain me* (Psalm 51:8-12).

In his state of rebellion and hardness, and under divine conviction, David could not experience the beautiful presence of God. Joy and gladness were gone, and he felt cast out of the Spirit's presence, as if his bones had been crushed by the Lord. Sin's pleasure can never compare with sin's pain. And so what does he pray? Once again, he pleads for complete and total forgiveness: "Lord, remove my sin so comprehensively that You cannot see it anymore, not even a trace of it!" And while we can debate whether we, as New Testament believers, should ask God to "create a pure heart" in us, because we have already been born from above, there can be no question about this—when you are under deep conviction from the Spirit, especially in times of revival, it truly feels like you are praying for a brand new heart.

But David doesn't stop there. He wants to be restored. He wants the joy back. He wants the intimacy back. He wants the holy presence back. *Restored joy is one of the great signs of forgiveness of sins.* That's why joy is so prevalent during times of revival. Sinners are getting saved—there is joy in heaven over this!—and believers are getting restored. There is no joy like revival joy.

> *Then I will teach transgressors your ways, so that sinners will turn back to you. Deliver me from the guilt of bloodshed, O God, you who are God my Savior, and my tongue will sing of your righteousness. Open my lips, Lord, and my mouth will declare your praise* (Psalm 51:13-15).

This reflects the heart of a broken and repentant believer. "When You restore me, I will restore others. When You forgive me, I will shout your offer of forgiveness to the world. I will not hold back! When You lift this terrible burden of crushing guilt—I have sinned so grievously, Lord!—I will sing aloud of Your goodness. My lips will shout praises to you!" As Jesus taught, the one who is forgiven much, loves much (see Luke 7:36-47).

> *You do not delight in sacrifice, or I would bring it; you do not take pleasure in burnt offerings. My sacrifice, O God, is a broken spirit; a broken and contrite heart you, God, will not despise* (Psalm 51:16-17).

These are remarkable words. David understood that God wanted his heart—a broken and contrite heart—rather than animal sacrifices, even though the Torah mandated animal sacrifices. He wanted David himself, crushed before the Lord with his own life offered up on the altar, rather than some religious routines.

Put another way, our Father wants *us*, not our tithes, not our fasting, not our pious rituals. He wants us to be living sacrifices, holy and acceptable to Him (see Rom. 12:1). He wants brokenness, not performance; He's looking for contrition, not accomplishments. Our Father will not despise a humble, shattered heart. As He said in Isaiah 57:15:

> *For this is what the high and exalted One says—he who lives forever, whose name is holy: "I live in a high and holy place, but also with the one who is contrite and lowly in spirit, to revive the*

> *spirit of the lowly and to revive the heart of the contrite."*

This does not mean self-condemnation. It does not mean that we walk around for months on end in depression and self-loathing. But it does mean that we are broken and humbled by a recognition of our sin, and rather than defend ourselves or blame others, we respond to the divine rebuke with honesty and humility: "I am guilty as charged, Lord! Have mercy on me! You are good and gracious, God, and you will not turn away the contrite. May the blood of Jesus cleanse me afresh!"

But there is still more to the psalm, and these closing verses most likely reflect the words of a later editor who added them—by the Spirit's inspiration—during the time of Babylonian exile, when the Temple lay in ruins.

> *May it please you to prosper Zion, to build up the walls of Jerusalem. Then you will delight in the sacrifices of the righteous, in burnt offerings offered whole; then bulls will be offered on your altar* (Psalm 51:18-19).

David's broken, sinful condition now stood as a picture for the nation as a whole, languishing in divine judgment in a foreign land. And the signs of judgment were evident, with the walls of Jerusalem broken down and the Temple sacrifices dormant. When the Lord restored the people and the city, then, in righteousness, they could come and offer their sacrifices. With their hearts restored, He would welcome their prayers, their fasting, their offerings.

That, too, is a fruit of revival—the favor of God is restored to the people and true worship is restored to the Temple. "Do it again in our day, Lord!" Let it start with you and with me.

Notes

1. Brown, *Hyper-Grace*, 69–90; more concisely, see idem, *The Grace Controversy: Answers to 12 Common Questions* (Lake Mary, FL: Charisma House, 2016), 57–68.
2. Some deny that David spoke here about the innate nature of human sinfulness—literally, from conception— arguing instead that this points to the fact that he himself was born out of wedlock, hence his mother conceived him in sin. But there is no textual or even traditional data to support this claim.

CHAPTER SIX

RESTORE MY FIRST LOVE!

Special Note: I began writing this chapter in September 2019, during a season of seeking the Lord for deep, personal renewal, wanting to put into writing what I was feeling, offering it up as a prayer to the Lord. It is open, raw, and vulnerable, and I share it here as I expressed it then. Perhaps your own heart will resonate with these words, especially if you are in full-time, vocational ministry?

Lord, I pray that You would restore me to my first love for You, to that time when being with You and worshiping You and feasting on Your Word was my greatest delight. Light that fire again!

I pray that You would bring me back to that time and place when intimacy was more important than ministry, when knowing You was more important than being known, when it didn't occur to me to be ashamed of You or to treat evangelism as a burden because I wanted everyone to know how wonderful You are. Turn me back, Lord!

Help me to remember the height from which I've fallen, to get a glimpse of how special and satisfying my fellowship with You used to be, to recall the indescribably glorious levels of joy I used to experience. Make it real to me again!

Help me to *love* prayer, to long for opportunities to get alone with You for hours (or days) on end, to delight in communion with You more than communion with any other person on the earth. That's what my heart longs for!

When I sang those old hymns in the first months and years of my faith, the words were so real to me, even though they were so culturally different than anything I had sung before. I think back to the words of one hymn when we would sing:

> *I come to the garden alone while*
> *the dew is still on the roses,*
> *And the voice I hear falling on my ear,*
> *The Son of God discloses*
> *And He walks with me and He talks with me,*
> *And He tells me I am his own;*

And the joy we share as we tarry there,
None other has ever known.

Father, that joy was so real!

And there was that Fanny Crosby hymn I so loved, "I Am Thine, O Lord," with one verse in particular being so precious to me:

O the pure delight of a single hour
That before Thy throne I spend,
When I kneel in prayer,
and with Thee, my God,
I commune as friend with friend!

It really was pure delight! And so, I pray the words of the chorus to that song again today, with all my heart and soul:

Draw me nearer, nearer, blessed Lord,
To the cross where Thou hast died;
Draw me nearer, nearer, nearer, blessed Lord,
To Thy precious, bleeding side.

Draw me nearer, Lord! Take my heart and ignite it again with that first love passion—but one that is deeper now, deepened by decades of knowing You, deepened by decades of experiencing Your faithfulness, deepened by decades of seeing my weakness and Your strength. Oh

Lord, for the end to be greater than the beginning and for the years ahead to be more glorious and wonderful than the years before! And for the cross to be so central in all I think and do.

But it is so easy for me to get caught up in *the work*—be it the burden to see this generation impacted or my heart for the salvation of Israel or the consuming call to write or running here or there for ministry—without being caught up *with You*. Abba! Bring me back to that place of worship, of adoration, of profound, inexpressible bliss simply in being Your child. May *You*—not ministry breakthroughs, not wonderful testimonies, not answers to prayer, not successful endeavors—be the greatest source of satisfaction in my life. You alone!

And bring me into an even deeper place of gazing on You like the twenty-four elders in Revelation, who continuously cry "Holy!" when they see You, who continuously cast their crowns at Your feet, who continuously are in awe of You. Strike me with that holy awe as well by revealing Yourself to me. What else matters?

Father, I remember Leonard Ravenhill telling me that the greatest quote he ever heard from A.W. Tozer was this: "There are occasions when for hours I lay prostrate before God without saying a word of prayer or praise—I just gaze on Him and worship." But this seems so, so out of reach. How do I get there?

I want to understand this kind of devotion for myself. I want to experience this while I live here in this world. I want to *really* see You and experience You and know You now in ways beyond anything I have ever seen or known. If not now, when?

But I often feel so superficial, so distracted, so on the run, so shallow. Deepen me, Father! And as I have prayed hundreds or thousands of times, so I pray again: Break my heart with the things that break Your heart. Shatter my indifference. Share Your burden with me! Help me to love what You love and hate what You hate. Help me to be one with You. It is possible, Father!

More Prayers from the Depths of My Heart

These are some of the specific prayers I journaled during this season as well, also reflecting a lighter travel schedule during some of this time:

> *Abba, cause my heart to burn with holy, undying, passionate love for **You**!*
>
> *Be glorified to the absolute maximum possible in my life, Lord! **Your glory** is what I seek!*
>
> *Abba, don't let me lose what You are doing in my heart these days! Nothing matters more than intimacy with **You**! As I get super busy, help me to put first things first! Matthew 6:33!*

> *Father, share Your heart with me! Let me burn and yearn with holy jealousy—for Your glory and for Your lost creation.*
>
> *God, get hold of **me**, from head to toe, inside and out, until I don't even recognize myself. Holy, like You, through and through.*
>
> *My identity must not be found in being busy but in being Your son, not in being productive but in being devoted, not in being known by man but being known by You. Oh, to be fully absorbed in God!*
>
> *Everything, everything, everything comes down to being rightly connected to the Head. All focus on King Jesus! All direction from Him! All wisdom and burdens and plans and insights and marching orders from Him!*

Then, after my schedule returned to its normal, super-busy intensity, I journaled this prayer: "Father, as I feared, with all the travel, writing, taping, local meetings, and more, I've gotten way too scattered. I'm spread *way* too thin—and I've neglected *You*. Abba, something must change long-term, and I plead for Your directives. Abba!"

And then, more prayers like this in the weeks that followed: "Lord, purify me! Refine me! Cleanse me thoroughly of everything unclean or unworthy in me—spirit, mind, heart, life, and body. Cause me to shine! Grant me deep and true repentance of anything that dishonors or displeases You. Make me like Your Son! Lord!"

And then this prayer, in the midst of the ministry busyness: "Father, give me a fresh, all-consuming vision of Your Son so that *He* rather than my calling or burden would be the all-consuming focus of my life. Lord!"

Then, late at night on the evening of February 25, 2020, en route to Australia immediately before the COVID-19 travel lockdown, while alone at JFK airport in New York, my heart was suddenly gripped:

> *Oh, my heart is bursting! Praying alone late at JFK, waiting for my Hong Kong flight, I get overwhelmed with pain for the world—just seeing a middle-aged man cleaning the carpets makes me think of how many people have it hard—and I tell the Lord I don't like pain. I just want everything to be nice. But I ask Him, once again, to let me share some of His pain, as long as He gives me the grace to carry it.*
>
> *Oh, this is intense! I'm also bursting—bursting!—with the agony of my calling. I cannot shake this burden. I cannot quench this fire. I must see You work through me until nations are shaken and Israel is saved. Father!*

Oh, the burden! Oh, the pain! **Something** *must happen.* **Something** *must shift. I* **must** *make the impact God has called me to make.* **Father!**

How the Lord marks us during times of encounter like this. How He takes us to a deeper place. How He impacts us for life. And how His calling burns in us until we are consumed with a passion to see His will come to pass in us and through us. Nothing matters more than that. Can you relate to these words?

In the months that followed, as my travel schedule stopped entirely for about five months because of COVID-19 (something I had not experienced in more than thirty-five years), I was jealous to seize the moment, pressing into the Lord. Yet even then, there were constant challenges to intimacy, as I prayed on April 3, 2020: "Father, even with no travel now because of the virus, I am once again running like crazy and hardly meeting with You. Abba, no more! Grab hold of me so deeply and intensely that for the rest of my life, all I will want is *You*."

Then, on April 15, 2020, this prayer: "Lord, during this shut down, this is the perfect opportunity for me to step higher, above the fray of everyday life, and get the bird's eye perspective—Your perspective—of my life and ministry. Help me, Lord, to seize this sacred moment! And give me clear marching orders for the future!"

Looking back now, more than one year from when I started journaling these prayers, I can say with certainty that God has been at work and that I have encountered Him more deeply in recent days than I have in many years. What a Savior! What a God! What love and goodness and truth and grace! How beautiful it has been to spend days alone with Him, worshiping at His feet and sobbing in His presence, overwhelmed by His power and beauty. He hears the cry of our hearts! He alone is what I desire. As we draw near to Him, He draws near to us—and we can be assured that it is He who is drawing us in the first place.

In the years ahead, I hope to experience the Lord so deeply that, as I have prayed many times, I will not even recognize myself. That's how powerful the renewed passion and devotion and love and commitment will be. That's how great the fresh revelation of the Lord will be. That's how comprehensive the personal transformation will be—and bear in mind that I write these words as a serious, committed, sold-out, unashamed, Jesus-loving believer, not as a compromised saint or, God forbid, a backslider. There is so much more to know of Him and to experience in Him. He is calling each of us deeper!

May the Lord light a fresh fire in you and me. May He restore us fully to our first love—and even more. May Jesus be glorified in our hearts and our minds like never before. Surely it is time!

CHAPTER SEVEN

SET THE TRUMPET TO YOUR MOUTH

We are living in urgent times, critical times, desperate times. We are living in times when the watchmen on the wall need to sound the alarm, stir the people of God, warn and exhort, and call to action. Instead, in so many of our churches and on so many of our social media outlets, the watchmen themselves are slumbering and lulling their people to sleep. How, then, can we awaken a dying world?

The truth be told, in church after church in America, in sermon after sermon and in teaching after teaching—on internet and TV and radio and social media and in books too many to count—we hear messages designed to make us feel comfortable, to make us feel good about

ourselves, to cause *us* to sleep. "All is well, little children, all is well!" Where is the sense of urgency?

In June 2019, a Christian publisher asked to me write an article on what I sensed the Spirit saying. I responded with this:

> As I pray and ask the Lord, "What is the Spirit saying?" I hear in my own spirit one word: urgency!
>
> These are urgent times, contentious times, confusing times.
>
> These are times of great upheaval and great opportunity.
>
> These are intense times, difficult times, blessed times.
>
> The Spirit is saying "Urgency!"
>
> Unfortunately, the message from all too many of our pulpits is not one of urgency. It is one of complacency. Of comfort. Of personal success.
>
> It is not a message designed to wake up a sleeping Church, not a message designed to prepare for war, not a message designed to challenge and stir.
>
> Instead, while moral confusion and spiritual deception rises, many of God's people are

enjoying a peaceful slumber, lulled to sleep by voices of compromise that refuse to confront sin, that refuse to address the culture, that refuse to talk about divine judgment.

It's time to wake up![1]

And I remind you: I wrote this in June 2019, a time that almost seems blissful and calm when compared to the tumultuous months that have followed.

I also cited this powerful quote from Catherine Booth (1829–1890) from her sermon "Aggressive Christianity." She said:

> "Opposition! It is a bad sign for the Christianity of this day that it provokes so little opposition. If there were no other evidence of it being wrong, I should know from that. When the Church and the world can jog along together comfortably, you may be sure there is something wrong. The world has not altered. Its spirit is exactly the same as it ever was, and if Christians were equally faithful and devoted to the Lord, and separated from the world, living so that their lives were a reproof to all ungodliness, the world would hate them as much as it ever did. It is the *Church* that has altered, *not* the world."

Yet today, in America, unless we push back against the sinful culture, the Church and the world jog together quite comfortably.

But it's not because we're changing the world. It's because the world is changing us. It's time that we wake up!

Kids are being exposed to pornography at 8 years old.

There are reportedly more witches in America than millennial Presbyterians.

Infanticide is being defended by elected officials.

Divisions are ripping our nation apart at the seams.

And the number of professing Christians in our country is decreasing rather than increasing.

How should we respond?

We live in a day in which, in a figure of speech, America is burning.

We should be burning too.

May God awaken His people! May He set our hearts ablaze. May He share His pain with us.

The Spirit is saying "Urgency!"[2]

Do you hear Him saying this as well?

We Are Living in Urgent Times

In the aftermath of the protests and riots of 2020, as some of our cities had literally been set ablaze, I tweeted this: "I truly believe that if more preachers were on fire then more believers would be on fire and less of our cities would be on fire."[3] Do you agree?

I hear voices from the past and from the present, shouting their words of warning, and my own spirit says, "Amen!"

I hear A.W. Tozer saying:

> Surely we need a baptism of clear seeing if we are to escape the fate of Israel (and of every other religious body in history that forsook God). If not the greatest need, then surely one of the greatest is for the appearance of Christian leaders with prophetic vision. We desperately need seers who can see through the mist. Unless they come soon, it will be too late for this generation. And if they do come, we will no doubt crucify a few of them in the name of our worldly orthodoxy. But the cross is always the harbinger of the resurrection.[4]

I hear Leonard Ravenhill saying, "We need a trumpet voice again to tell sluggish believers that God requires holiness of His people. *There is a famine of true holiness preaching.*"[5]

I hear Nicki Cruz saying,

> We stink more of the world than we stink of sackcloth and ashes. A lot of contemporary churches today would feel more at home in a movie house rather than in a house of prayer, more afraid of holy living than of sinning, know more about money than magnifying Christ in our bodies. It is so compromised that holiness and living a sin-free life is heresy to the modern church. The modern church is, quite simply, just the world with a Christian T-shirt on![6]

I believe the Spirit is saying, "Back to the cross. Back to the basics. Back to repentance. Back to truth-telling, however unpopular that may be. Back to the real Jesus and the real gospel." Is the Spirit speaking this to you as well?

Isaiah 58 begins with the words, "Shout it aloud, do not hold back. Raise your voice like a trumpet. Declare to my people their rebellion and to the descendants of Jacob their sins" (Isa. 58:1). Similarly, God said to the prophet Hosea, "Set the trumpet to thy mouth. He shall come as an eagle against the house of the Lord, because they have transgressed my covenant, and trespassed against my law" (Hos. 8:1 KJV).

Those words, "Set the trumpet to thy mouth," became the title of David Wilkerson's 1985 book, a book filled with prophetic rebukes and dire warnings. (I'll talk about this book in more depth in Chapter Ten.) Leonard Ravenhill wrote the foreword to the book, which is worth quoting at length:

> Dr. [Warren] Wiersbe has given us a lovely book on walking with the giants. Brother David has given us something better than that in this wonderful book, and it is walking with the prophets.
>
> There is probably no preacher in the nation who is more intimate and knowledgeable on the crime and accelerated depravity in the inner cities of our nation, but he skillfully avoids any horrendous statistics on these youth-crippling vices, which is the result of the anemic preaching of the Word of the living God. There is so little preaching of Christ, repentance, and judgment of sin.

What a piercing indictment—the decadent and depraved state of the nation is, in some part, "the result of the anemic preaching of the Word of the living God."

He continues:

> Often I am asked, Is David Wilkerson a prophet? Well, not in the classification of the Old Testament, but surely a prophet in the bracket of the New Testament. I claim for him that God has made him a watchman unto our nation. My slight contribution to this book is like a man taking a bucket of fire and adding it to a volcano, for this book certainly is volcanic. The author sees the church of Jesus Christ wounded, raped, and robbed; and he blows God's trumpet to show us the sin and unbelief that caused it.
>
> He has been broken in compassion for the weak and withered testimony of believers today in a world of arrogant heresy and strident cults. I saw him on one occasion stagger into my office, and his lips trembled as he spoke with tears in his eyes, saying, "Len, I hardly dare put on paper and publish what the Lord has given to me." But he has done this, and I for one am tremendously glad that he did.

These words, too, are jolting—Wilkerson sees "the church of Jesus Christ wounded, raped, and robbed." How much of this, too, is the result of "anemic preaching"?

How much damage has been done by our pep-talk, carnal-prosperity, "what's in it for me" message? What really happens when we fail to sound the alarm or speak the truth in love?

Ravenhill wrote:

> The book will bring a cry of joy from the young preachers who are asking for a spiritual voice compelling the church back to her original calling of holiness and power. The author has followed the command of Joel to "Blow the trumpet in Zion, and sound an alarm in my holy mountain...A divine intervention is our only hope. This trumpet gives no uncertain sound."[7]

To be sure, we have had more than enough doomsday messages. We have had more than enough date-setters who wrongly predicted the end of the world and put God's people in a panic. I have even heard of godly families relocating to other parts of America (or the world) based on prophecies of imminent divine judgment and calamity, none of which, to date, have come to pass.

The last thing I'm advocating is that Christian leaders work God's people into a frenzy with fear-based, sensationalistic preaching. God forbid. Nor do I believe we should confuse an Old Testament message with a New

Testament message, as if God deals with the believing Church in exactly the same way He dealt with unbelieving Israel.[8] I am certainly not talking about bashing God's people over the head with a Bible.

Urgency is not the same as condemnation. Warning is not the same as hopelessness. Passion is not the same as hysteria. But we have gone from setting the trumpet to our mouths and sounding the alarm to playing lullabies and hitting the snooze button. As one of my friends recently said to me, many of our churches seem to be promoting "spa Christianity"!

The Trumpet of the Lord

In the Book of Revelation, when John heard Jesus speak, this is what he wrote: "On the Lord's Day I was in the Spirit, and I heard behind me *a loud voice like a trumpet*, which said: 'Write on a scroll what you see and send it to the seven churches: to Ephesus, Smyrna, Pergamum, Thyatira, Sardis, Philadelphia and Laodicea'" (Rev. 1:10-11, my emphasis).

John then records this:

> *I turned around to see the voice that was speaking to me. And when I turned I saw seven golden lampstands, and among the lampstands was someone like a son of man, dressed in a robe*

*reaching down to his feet and with a golden sash around his chest. The hair on his head was white like wool, as white as snow, and his eyes were like blazing fire. His feet were like bronze glowing in a furnace, and **his voice was like the sound of rushing waters**. In his right hand he held seven stars, and **coming out of his mouth was a sharp, double-edged sword**. His face was like the sun shining in all its brilliance* (Revelation 1:12-16, my emphasis).

And as Jesus delivered His messages to the seven churches of Asia Minor, the most "prophetic" words in the New Testament in terms of God speaking to His people, the Lord said this: "Whoever has ears, let them hear what the Spirit says to the churches" (Rev. 3:22). This one whose voice sounded like a trumpet, like the sound of rushing waters, and from whose mouth was a sharp, double-edged sword was the one delivering the Spirit's words. That voice like a trumpet must be heard again today, right within the Church.

It is a voice that will stir us and move us, a voice that will awaken us and call us, a voice that will penetrate to the very depths of our being, producing lasting, radical change. We need to hear the trumpet blast again. Otherwise, there will be nothing to stop our slide into moral chaos and cultural anarchy. We are well on the way there now.

I recognize that not everyone is called to bring a prophetic message. I understand that some are called to teach the Word in depth while others are called to bring encouragement and hope. I esteem the different callings and anointings in the Body, and I know that we need each other desperately.

I also categorically reject a faultfinding, holier-than-thou spirit, and I reject the spirit of hyper-criticism.[9] I reject a graceless message that tears down without building up. Even when our hearts are bursting with a recognition of the church's sin and a revelation of the holiness of God—as Ezekiel received in the first three chapters of his book—we are only to speak as the Spirit directs. As the Lord said to Ezekiel, whom He had appointed as a watchman, called to sound the alarm:

> *Then the Spirit came into me and raised me to my feet. He spoke to me and said: "Go, shut yourself inside your house. And you, son of man, they will tie with ropes; you will be bound so that you cannot go out among the people. I will make your tongue stick to the roof of your mouth so that you will be silent and unable to rebuke them, for they are a rebellious people. But when*

I speak to you, I will open your mouth and you shall say to them, 'This is what the Sovereign Lord says.' Whoever will listen let them listen, and whoever will refuse let them refuse; for they are a rebellious people" (Ezekiel 3:24-27).

We speak His burden, not ours, and we do it by the Spirit, not out of human frustration or judgmentalism. When we speak in the flesh, we do more harm than good, however "righteous" our message might be.

I'm simply saying this: Many of our watchmen are not on the alert. Many of our leaders have sold out to the spirit of the age. Many of our pastors have become entertainers and performers. Many of our teachers tell us what our itching ears need to hear. As one Old Testament scholar stated, "The false prophet...makes things easier for his listeners."[10] Exactly.

This is not the Spirit of God. This is not the voice of Jesus. This is not the heart of the Father. *Something is sorely missing.* The boat is capsizing while the captain is cracking jokes. Where, I ask again, is our sense of urgency?

How many more scandals must we endure until we recognize that something is very wrong? (I do not say this to condemn those who have fallen, understanding that there but for the grace of God go I. I simply say this to point out that we need revival urgently.) How much more does the sin of the world need to contaminate the Church of God before we awake? At what point do our leaders get gripped and stir the Body out of complacency?

An executive pastor in a mega-church in California told me that all his children, who are now adults, differ with his views on homosexuality. They were raised in a godly home and were taught the Word but have been more influenced by their peers and the society in which they live. This is becoming increasingly common.

Concerned Christian parents reach out to me all the time with similar stories, "My teenaged daughter believes she's a boy and wants to transition. What do I say? We dedicated her to Jesus when she was born." Or, "We found out during the COVID-19 lockdown that our daughter has developed a lesbian relationship with another teen online. She listens to worship music, we pray with her, but she feels this is fine in God's sight. What do we do?"

Josh McDowell has said publicly that the objections to the Bible and the Christian faith that he used to deal with on college campuses are now common among kids as young as twelve or thirteen. Does this concern us? Are we alarmed?

In his book *The Last Christian Generation*, McDowell writes, "The Christian faith has been under attack in this culture for decades and because most believers haven't been equipped to know why they believe, the very foundation of Christianity within the Church has eroded. If trends continue, the next generation of the Church will not even be rightfully called Christian."[11] He wrote this in 2006!

In 2010, Christian thinker Os Guinness wrote a spy novel titled, *The Last Christian on Earth: Uncover the Enemy's Plot to Undermine the Church*.[12] Then, in 2018, he wrote another book with a provocative title: *Last Call for Liberty: How America's Genius for Freedom Has Become Its Greatest Threat*.[13] Note again that operative word "last." Note also that, in all that I've written here, I've not said a word about cancel culture, about mobocracy, about the rising tide of socialism, about a stifling politically correct spirit, about the very real threat to our most fundamental freedoms. There is so much to be said about all this![14]

The hour really is urgent, and it is a time for pastors and leaders and prophets and teachers and apostles and evangelists to put the trumpet to their mouths. With a broken heart before God, with a passionate love for Jesus, with compassion for a hurting bride and a dying world, and with the Spirit of God upon you, the Lord will give you words to say. They might just save a generation from catastrophe.

Set the trumpet to your mouth!

Notes

1. See Michael Brown, "Why the Holy Spirit Is Crying 'Urgency!' to Today's Sleeping Church," Charisma News, November 3, 2019, https://www.charismanews.com/opinion/78644-why-the-holy-spirit-is-crying-urgency-to-today-s-sleeping-church.

2. Ibid. For the Catherine Booth quote, see Catherine Booth, *The Writings of Catherine Booth: Aggressive Christianity* (n.p.: Salvation Army, 1986), 11.

3. Michael Brown, Twitter @DrMichaelLBrown, October 30, 2020, https://twitter.com/DrMichaelLBrown/status/1322240226736148480.

4. A.W. Tozer, "From Spiritual Infancy to Maturity," https://www.cmalliance.org/devotions/tozer?id=886.

5. I heard this firsthand from Leonard Ravenhill, with whom I was close friends from 1989–1994, as mentioned here in this book.

6. See https://www.inspiringquotes.us/author/1250-nicky-cruz.

7. Leonard Ravenhill, "Introduction," in David Wilkerson, *Set the Trumpet to Thy Mouth* (Lindale, TX: World Challenge, 1985), n.p.

8. There are lessons to learn from the Old Testament, along with many important parallels; see, for example, Romans 15:4 and 1 Corinthians 10:1-12. But, again, there are differences as well, because of the cross.

9. For a description of destructive criticism, see Michael L. Brown, *The Revival Answer Book* (Ventura, CA: Renew Books, 2001), 47–83; this is the revised edition of *Let*

No One Deceive You: Confronting the Critics of Revival (Shippensburg, PA: Destiny Image, 1997). See also idem, *From Holy Laughter to Holy Fire*, 27–66.

10. Hans Walter Wolff, cited in Elmer A. Maartens, "Jeremiah: Relevant for the Eighties," *Direction*, Spring, 1986, https://directionjournal.org/15/1/jeremiah-relevant -for-eighties.html.

11. Josh McDowell, *The Last Christian Generation* (Grand Rapids: Baker Books, 2006), cited in the product description of the book.

12. Os Guinness, *The Last Christian on Earth: Uncover the Enemy's Plot to Undermine the Church* (Grand Rapids: Baker Books, 2010).

13. Os Guiness, *Last Call for Liberty: How America's Genius for Freedom Has Become Its Greatest Threat* (Downers Grove, IL: InterVarsity Press, 2018).

14. See again Brown, *Jezebel's War with America*; idem, *Revolution: An Urgent Call to a Holy Uprising* (second, revised edition; Lake Mary, FL: Charisma House, 2020).

CHAPTER EIGHT

DO YOU NOT KNOW THAT YOUR HONOR IS AT STAKE?

Revival is often birthed when we get to a place of spiritual desperation, when we are sick and tired of the way we are living, when we have had it with our halfhearted commitments, when we cannot live any longer without a breakthrough. That has been a theme of this book from the opening chapter until now.

Revival can also come when we are grieved and burdened over the state of the society, when the sins of our generation mount up to heaven and we know that judgment is near. That also drives us to our knees in intercession and repentance, leading to an outpouring of mercy from on high. This, too, has been a theme throughout this book.

But there is something else that can spark revival, something else that moves us to prayer and grips us with deep travail: jealousy for the reputation of the Lord. Our hearts are broken because our Master's name is maligned. Our souls are grieved because the people of the world despise their Creator. And it is all because of us. The Lord's name is mocked because of our failures, because of our poor witness, because of our sins and divisions and scandals. His perfect name is degraded because we, His children, make Him look bad.

Jesus gave His life for a rebellious race, sacrificing Himself so unworthy sinners could live. Yet we drive those very sinners away from Him by our compromised conduct and loose living. Isn't this enough to break your heart?

Leonard Ravenhill touched on this when he wrote, "The true man of God is heartsick, grieved at the worldliness of the Church, grieved at the blindness of the Church, grieved at the corruption in the Church, grieved at the toleration of sin in the Church, grieved at the prayerlessness in the Church. He is disturbed that the corporate prayer of the Church no longer pulls down the strongholds of the devil."[1] And he is grieved because we have misrepresented the Lord.

I had the privilege of praying with Leonard Raven-hill many times, and his prayers were on an entirely different level than anything I had ever heard or experienced. There was such depth and devotion and passion and precision. To pray with him was to go into the holiest place of all.

But we not only prayed together when I would stay at his house for a few days each year (I did this for the last five years of his life). He also had set times each day when he would get alone, and so, in the afternoon, no matter what company he had at his house, he would excuse himself to meet with the Lord. It was an appointment he would not break.

Virtually every time I stayed with him, the pattern would repeat itself. Brother Len would break away for his afternoon prayer time and then, an hour or two later, he would come out of his room completely undone. "Mike," he would say to me, with tears in his eyes and anguish in his voice, "the Bride is naked and she doesn't even know it. I'm so ashamed."

He was so in love with Jesus that it shattered him to think His Bride was in such poor condition, in particular in America. And this moved him to unceasing prayer for revival, because a revived Church would be a glorious Church, a beautiful Church, a Church worthy of her Savior, a Bride suitable for her Groom. A revived Church would bring honor, not reproach, to the name of her Lord.

It was the anguished prayers of Ravenhill that moved him to write words like this:

> Could a mariner sit idle if he heard the drowning cry?
>
> Could a doctor sit in comfort and just let his patients die?
>
> Could a fireman sit idle, let men burn and give no hand?
>
> Can you sit at ease in Zion with the world around you damned?[2]

Is your own heart stirred as you read? Does something deep within you long for a deeper walk with God? Have you had it with our superficial spirituality and our casual Christianity? Oh that the Lord would share His burden with us! Edward Payson (1787–1823), known as "Praying Payson of Portland," expressed it like this: "I do not believe that my desires for revival were ever half so strong as they ought to be; nor do I see how a minister can help being in a 'constant fever'...where His Master is dishonored and souls are destroyed in so many ways."

Yet here in America, where our Master is so dishonored and souls are destroyed in so many ways, so many of us are nonchalant, casual, and unconcerned—really anything but living *in a constant fever*—and this applies to many of us who are called to be leaders in the Church.

We have so little anguish. We carry so little burden. Our messages are so often lightweight, calculated to entertain rather than to convict. As for our prayers, how often do we cry out with sobbing and tears? How often do our hearts burst with the pain of a dying world? Whatever happened to brokenness? Whatever happened to anguish? Whatever happened to holy jealousy?

Listen to this impassioned cry from David Wilkerson, taken from a message he preached September 15, 2002. He asked:

> Whatever happened to anguish in the house of God? Whatever happened to anguish in the ministry? It's a word you don't hear in this pampered age. You don't hear it. Anguish means extreme pain and distress. The emotions so stirred that it becomes painful, acute deeply felt inner pain, because of conditions about you, in you, or around you. Anguish, deep pain, deep sorrow, and agony of God's heart.

He continued:

> All true passion is born out of anguish. All true passion for Christ comes out of a baptism of anguish. You search the scripture and you'll find that when God determined to recover a

ruined situation, he would seek out a praying man, and he'd take him down into the waters of anguish. He would share his own anguish for what God saw happening to his church and to his people, and he would find a praying man, and he would take that man and literally baptize him in anguish.[3]

The Prayer That Shook an Island

It was this kind of anguish, this kind of jealousy for the honor of the Lord that helped bring about a dramatic breakthrough in the parish of Arnol during the Hebrides Revival (1949–1952). In the months prior to visitation in Arnol:

People on the island [of Lewis] were inexplicably drawn to Christ. Without publicity, telephones, or Internet, they awoke in the middle of the night and felt compelled to gather in a farmer's field or at a local parish church. Sometimes they did not make it—and instead simply fell by the side of the road, confessing their sins to God. Bars and dance halls shut their doors for good. Starting with the small town of Barvas, the entire Isle of Lewis turned from darkness to light. Entire towns were being converted to Christ, with the exception of the stubborn little parish of Arnol.

Arnol defiantly resisted the gospel. No one wanted to hear what Duncan Campbell [the principle leader used during the revival] had to say. In fact, the citizenry held opposition meetings to denounce the revival. Campbell and his fellow leaders knew the only answer was prayer.[4]

Yes, leaders from Scotland were actually brought in to Arnol to preach against Campbell and the revival, hardening the people there to what the Spirit was doing. And so the revival hit a brick wall with the local people there. We'll let Campbell tell the rest of the sacred story. Speaking of these opposition ministers, he said:

Well, they came, and they were so successful in their opposition that very few people from this particular community came near any of my meetings. It is true that the church was crowded, it is true that people were standing outside that couldn't get in, but these were people who came from neighboring parishes. Brought by coaches, brought by cars and what have you—but there were very few from this particular village.

So one night one of the elders came to me and said, "Mr. Campbell, there is only one thing that we can do. We must give ourselves to prayer—give ourselves to prayer. Prayer changes things."

Well you know I am very willing for that. I said, "Where will we meet?" "Oh," he said, "There is a farmer and he is very willing to place his farmhouse at our disposal."

It was winter and the church was cold. There was no heating in it. The people believe in a crowded church to provide its own heat. But here we wanted a warmer spot, and the farmer was approached.

Interestingly, the farmer wasn't a Christian, but a God-fearing man with a Christian background. So he was happy to open his house for prayer. Campbell relates:

I would say there were about 30 of us including five ministers of the church of Scotland. Men who had burdens—longings to see God move in revival. And we were praying and oh, the going was hard. At least I felt it hard.

...We prayed till twelve or one o'clock in the morning when I turned again to the black-smith. Oh, he was a prince in the parish. And

I said to him, "John, I feel that God would have me to call upon you to pray." He had been silent up till then. And that dear man began. ...Half an hour he prayed, then he paused for a second or so, and looking up to the heavens he cried, "God, did you know that your honor is at stake? Your honor is at stake! You promised to pour floods upon the dry ground and, God, you're not doing it!"

That was the great burden of his heart—the honor of God was at stake. This man was jealous for the reputation of the Lord, and he was convinced that God had given the people a promise from Isaiah 44 that He would pour out His Spirit on the Hebrides—yet He was not doing it. This was a matter of the Lord's honor. Would He or would He not keep His word? Campbell continues:

My dear people, could we pray like that? Ah, but here was a man who could. Here was a man who could. Then he went on to say this: "There are five ministers in this meeting and I don't know where a one of them stands in your presence, not even Mr. Campbell. [Oh, he was an honest man.] But if I know my own poor heart, I think I can say and I think that you know that I'm thirsty! I'm thirsty to see the devil defeated in this parish. I'm thirsty to see this community gripped as you gripped Barvas! I'm longing for revival and, God, you're not doing it! And I'm thirsty and you've promised to pour water on me." Then a pause, and then he cried, "God, I now take upon myself to challenge you to fulfill your covenant engagement!" Now it was nearing two o'clock in the morning.

What a holy prayer! And what an incredibly bold prayer, the kind of prayer that only a broken-hearted, faith-filled believer could pray. How did the Lord respond to this challenge? Once again, we'll let Campbell describe it in his own words, as he was there to see it.

And what happened? The house shook. A jug on a sideboard fell onto the floor and broke. A minister beside me said, "An earth tremor!" And I said, "Yes, Murdo," but I had my own thoughts: my mind went back to the Acts, chapter four, when they prayed the place was shaken. When John Smith [the blacksmith] finished praying at twenty minutes past two, I pronounced the benediction and left the house. What did I see? The whole community alive! Men carrying chairs, women carrying stools and asking, "Is there room for us in the churches?" And the Arnol Revival broke out. And oh, what a sweeping revival! I believe there wasn't a single house in the village that wasn't shaken by God.

And this is now taking place in the middle of the night, as the community is being stirred by the holy presence of God, only hours after ignoring the very meeting where Campbell had been preaching. The Lord Himself was jealous for His honor. Campbell continues:

> I went into another farmhouse. I was thirsty, I was tired, I was needing something to drink, and I went in to ask for a glass of milk and I found nine women in the kitchen crying to God for mercy. Nine of them! The power of God swept. And there was a little boy, and he's kneeling and he's crying to God for mercy. And one of the elders goes over to him and prays over him, and little Donald MacPhail... came to know the Savior, and I believe more were led to Christ by that young lad than through the preaching of all of the ministers on the island together.[5]

And that is only the beginning of the story. God was jealous for His name and for His honor, jealous for the wellbeing of His people, jealous to see satan vanquished and souls liberated, and so He broke through dramatically in Arnol. He wants to share that holy jealously with us. He wants us to get to that place of intimacy so that we cry out with that blacksmith, "God, do You know that Your honor is at stake? Do You know that Your honor is at stake? You promised to pour water on the thirsty and floods on the dry ground and, God, You are not doing it." What about Your honor, Lord?

When God's Name Is Blasphemed Because of Us

Look at what is written in Isaiah 52:

> For this is what the Sovereign Lord says: "At first my people went down to Egypt to live; lately, Assyria has oppressed them. And now what do I have here?" declares the Lord. "For my people have been taken away for nothing, and those who rule them mock," declares the Lord. "And all day long my name is constantly blasphemed (Isaiah 52:4-5).

God sent His people into exile because of their sin, yet when they languished in exile, with the Temple in Jerusalem destroyed, it made the Lord, Israel's God, look bad. Yahweh's people were living as captives in a foreign land, with their God apparently defeated by the gods of the nations. The house of the one true God lay in ruins, while the idol temples were thriving. Consequently, the Lord's name was constantly blasphemed.

What was His solution? "Therefore my people will know my name; therefore in that day they will know that it is I who foretold it. Yes, it is I" (Isa. 52:6). He would reveal Himself to His people, deliver them from exile, restore them to their land, and visit them with His presence. Then the nations would know that the God of Israel was the only true God. He would vindicate His name before the world.

This same theme is repeated in Ezekiel 36 against a similar backdrop of the Jewish people languishing in Babylonian exile. The prophet declared:

> *Again the word of the Lord came to me: "Son of man, when the people of Israel were living in their own land, they defiled it by their conduct and their actions. Their conduct was like a woman's monthly uncleanness in my sight. So I poured out my wrath on them because they had shed blood in the land and because they had defiled it with their idols. I dispersed them among the nations, and they were scattered through the countries; I judged them according*

to their conduct and their actions. And wherever they went among the nations they profaned my holy name, for it was said of them, 'These are the Lord's people, and yet they had to leave his land.' I had concern for my holy name, which the people of Israel profaned among the nations where they had gone" (Ezekiel 36:16-21).

The judgment of God upon His sinning people brought reproach and dishonor to His holy name. And so, for the sake of His own reputation, He restored His exiled people—not because they deserved it, but for His name's sake:

Therefore say to the Israelites, "This is what the Sovereign Lord says: It is not for your sake, people of Israel, that I am going to do these things, but for the sake of my holy name, which you have profaned among the nations where you have gone. I will show the holiness of my great name, which has been profaned among the nations, the name you have profaned among them. Then the nations will know that I am the Lord, declares the Sovereign Lord, when I am proved holy through you before their eyes" (Ezekiel 36:22-23)

What's more, He said that He would display His holiness by making His people holy, giving them a new heart and a new spirit, writing His laws on their minds, cleansing them from sin, and causing them to dwell securely in the land (see Ezek. 36:24-28).

This cycle is being repeated in front of our eyes as a compromised, carnal, complacent church is bringing reproach to our Savior's name. This should lead us to a holy jealousy for His honor, which in turn will move God to act for His name's sake. A revived people will bring Him glory before a watching world.

The prophet Isaiah speaks to this as well, sharing his devastation and pain over the destruction that was about to come on his people. He cried out, "Therefore I said, 'Turn away from me; let me weep bitterly. Do not try to console me over the destruction of my people'" (Isa. 22:4). Commenting on this verse, John Calvin wrote:

> Here the Prophet, in order to affect more deeply the hearts of the Jews, assumes the character of a mourner, and not only so, but bitterly bewails the distressed condition of the Church of God [by which Calvin means God's ancient people Israel]. This passage must not be explained in the same manner as some former passages, in which he described the grief and

sorrow of foreign nations; but he speaks of the fallen condition of the Church of which he is a member, and therefore he sincerely bewails it, and invites others by his example to join in the lamentation. *What has befallen the Church ought to affect us in the same manner as if it had befallen each of us individually; for otherwise what would become of that passage? "The zeal of thy house hath eaten me up."* (Psalm 69:9.)[6]

Do you grasp the significance of these words? God's burden becomes our burden to the point that "what has befallen the Church" affects us "in the same manner as if it had befallen each of us individually." This is what the psalmist meant when he wrote that zeal for God's house consumed him. This same zeal consumed Jesus, as the disciples came to realize (see John 2:13-17). He burned with passion for the purity and honor of His Father's house.

It was in this same spirit that Arthur W. Pink (1886–1952) wrote: "O that we were more deeply moved by the languishing state of Christ's cause upon the earth today, by the inroads of the enemy and the awful desolation he has wrought in Zion! Alas that a spirit of indifference, or at least of fatalistic stoicism, is freezing so many of us."[7] Or, as expressed by my dear friend Art Katz (1929–2007), "A church with apostolic foundations is that body of people whose central impulse and principle of life, being and service is one thing only, namely, a radical and total jealousy for the glory of God."[8]

In a word, that is the message of this chapter. May it drive us to our knees with holy prayers that bleed. As J.H. Jowett (1863–1923) said, "As soon as we cease to bleed, we cease to bless."[9]

In his classic song "Asleep in the Light," Keith Green raised this plaintive cry:

> *Do you see? Do you see?*
> *All the people sinking down?*
> *Don't you care? Don't you care?*
> *Are you gonna let them drown?*
> *How can you be so numb?!*
> *Not to care if they come*
> *You close your eyes*
> *And pretend the job's done.*[10]

Yes, how can we be so numb?

If the Lord does not return for some years, I believe future generations of Christians will not be so shocked when they look at the moral collapse of the society in our time. Instead, as they survey the books we were reading, the sermons we were hearing, and the movies we were watching, they will ask, "What were they thinking?

How could these multiplied tens of millions of Christians be so indifferent while America unraveled?"

We live in a day in which, in a figure of speech, America is burning. We should be burning too.

May God awaken His people! May He set our hearts ablaze. May He share His pain with us. May we be consumed with a holy jealousy for His holy name. And may He arise and revive His people, thereby glorifying His Son. Let His people say Amen!

Notes

1. Leonard Ravenhill, *Revival God's Way* (Bloomington, MN: Bethany House Publishers, 1983), 69.
2. See http://christian-quotes.ochristian.com/Leonard -Ravenhill-Quotes/page-2.shtml.
3. David Wilkerson, "A Call to Anguish," September 15, 2002, https://www.sermonindex.net/modules/articles/index.php?view=article&aid=32622.
4. Jim Jarman, "When God Answered the Prayers of a Scotsman," Supernatural Movement of God, https://onecry.com/uncategorized/when-god-answered-the -prayers-of-a-scotsman.
5. Duncan Campbell, *Revival in the Hebrides* (Kraus House Digital Media, 2015), https://books.google.com/books?id=pKBhCwAAQBAJ&printsec=frontcover #v=onepage&q=%22successful%20in%20their %20opposition%22&f=false.

6. Available online at https://biblehub.com/commentaries/calvin/isaiah/22.htm, my emphasis.

7. Arthur W. Pink, *The Life of Elijah* (Zeeland, MI: Reformed Church Publications, 2017), https://books.google.com/books?id=5p86DwAAQBAJ&printsec=frontcover#v=onepage&q=%22languishing%20state%22&f=false.

8. Art Katz, *Apostolic Foundations: The Challenge of Living an Authentic Christian Life* (Burning Bush Publications, 2000), 5; https://static1.squarespace.com/static/57c0c4de6a4963efc2b89f72/t/58a77399725e25c4fa9f281e/1487369114542/Apostolic+Foundations+-+Katz+PDF.pdf.

9. J.H. Jowett, *The School of Calvary & The Passion For Souls: Sharing His Suffering* (Radford, VA: Christ Church—Radford Publications), 89; reprinted from the original, James Clarke and Company, London, 1911.

10. See https://genius.com/Keith-green-asleep-in-the-light-lyrics. To see Keith seeing this song live, see https://www.youtube.com/watch?v=em5gL0Rw4Aw.

CHAPTER NINE

CELEBRITY CHRISTIANITY, SUPERSTAR SAINTS, AND POLITICAL PROPHETS

As much as Christianity has dwindled in recent decades in America, there has also been much success and growth. None of this is more visible than in our mega-churches, with multiple congregations numbering in the tens of thousands. Some of these churches gather in immense, beautiful, mega-expensive buildings, complete with the latest and best technology and the finest accoutrements, from fancy coffee shops in the lobby to first-class gyms in the basement.

But I do not say this to be critical. I have preached in some of these churches and I have been blessed to see a real love for worship and a genuine honor for the Word of God. I rejoice in their success and do not belittle their numbers. To the contrary, some of these churches are doing much good in their local communities, helping the poor and the needy, reaching out to the lost, and sending millions of dollars to support overseas missions. I truly thank God for the good they are doing.

Other churches and leaders have massive TV and radio and internet ministries, with tens of millions of followers and viewers worldwide. Here too I rejoice if the Lord, indeed, has given them growth and favor. May His name be exalted through them.

At the same time, it is very easy to be misled by numbers, to be impressed by outward appearances, to be seduced by crowds and wealth, to measure things by human standards rather than by the standards of God. All that glitters is not gold, and often what is highly esteemed among people is an abomination in the sight of God (see Luke 16:15; this is what Jesus said.) Sometimes we have turned things completely upside down.

Quantity is great, but not at the expense of quality. Numbers are wonderful, but only when they represent real disciples. Prosperity is a blessing, as long as it is not a goal or a measure or a trap. Success is terrific, but only if it comes because of obedience rather than compromise. As Paul himself warned:

By the grace God has given me, I laid a foundation as a wise builder, and someone else is building on it. But each one should build with care. For no one can lay any foundation other than the one already laid, which is Jesus Christ. If anyone builds on this foundation using gold, silver, costly stones, wood, hay or straw, their work will be shown for what it is, because the Day will bring it to light. It will be revealed with fire, and the fire will test the quality of each person's work. If what has been built survives, the builder will receive a reward. If it is burned up, the builder will suffer loss but yet will be saved—even though only as one escaping through the flames (1 Corinthians 3:10-15).

What a shame it will be if, on that great day, all our work goes up in flames as the fire reveals our pride, our ambition, our manipulation, our fleshly performances. What a shame it will be if the words of Jesus, rebuking the hypocritical religious leaders of His day, will be found to apply to us: "Everything they do is done for people to see" (Matt. 23:5). Does that describe you or me?

Whatever Happened to the Power of the Spirit?

On December 1, 2020, I tweeted, "In the New Testament Church, the leaders were marked by purity of life, devotion to the cross, the power of the Spirit, and perseverance in the midst of persecution. Many of our church leaders today are marked by slick outfits, slick presentations, and slick marketing slogans."[1] Do you think I'm exaggerating?

I'm all for being physically fit. (Since when is being fat or dressing like a slob a sign of holiness?) I'm all for staying current. (Why use a typewriter when you can use a laptop? And why record your messages on cassette tapes if no one today owns a cassette player?) And there's nothing sacred about church names like "First Assembly." (One of the young men I help mentor has a really cool—and biblically based—name for his congregation. Why not?)

My issue is the idea that being cool has somehow become a Christian ideal, that being relevant now takes the place of being anointed, that knowing what is trending is equal to knowing the voice of the Spirit. To the contrary, this is nothing less than the wisdom of the world and the power of the flesh. And I can assure you that an old-fashioned preacher using a King James Bible and wearing an out of style three-piece suit, but anointed with the fire of God and flowing in the power of God, would get more done in one week than our celebrity preachers get done in one year. The truth be told, we have gone from consecration to commercialism and from surrender to sophistication. Am I not telling the truth?

Where is the evidence of the power and presence of God in our ministries and our lives? What are we doing that could not be done without the supernatural grace of the Spirit? Where is His demonstration in our midst? And why is it that the early Church could do nothing without the power and presence of the Spirit, and that the persecuted Church worldwide knows that it can do nothing without the power and presence of the Spirit, but we have managed to figure out how to do everything without that same power and presence?

Who changed the formula? Who came up with a new secret code? How is it that we now know better than Jesus and Paul and the anointed saints of past generations? Or could it be that we have become so accustomed to the absence of the Spirit that we don't even realize that He is gone? As I wrote in *It's Time to Rock the Boat*:

> Oh yes, it's easy to be "busy" for the Lord, running here and there, going to meetings and special events, counseling, preaching, teaching, raising funds, doing good works, "ministering" with all of our might for Jesus. But let the whole truth be told! Much of our ministry

today is a concerted, sometimes frantic attempt to make up for the absence of the Spirit. We are trying instead of tarrying, working instead of waiting, doing instead of dying, sweating instead of seeking. Our "spiritual" ministry reeks of the flesh. *What the Lord does is holy, holy, holy; what we do is hollow, hollow, hollow.*[2]

But lest you think I'm pointing a finger at others, I'm also preaching to myself (although, to be candid, I have never had to worry about looking slick!) I can do a good radio show because I'm a natural talker. I can win a debate using my intellect and skills. I can impart all kinds of wisdom on difficult theological topics based on my years of study. I can respond to the secular critics and the hostile mockers having had lots of personal experience sitting in the hot seat. And I can do all this without the power of the Spirit and not even notice He is missing.

That's why I have often fallen on my face in prayer and cried out to the Lord with passion and brokenness, "Lord, where is the demonstration of Your Spirit in my ministry? Where is the evidence that Jesus has risen from the dead in my own personal life?"

It's not that I am primarily called to be a healing evangelist, curing the sick and raising the dead. That is not my specific divine gifting. And it's not that I want to change the name of my radio show from *The Line of Fire* to *The Miracle Hour of Power*. That is not why the Lord has me on the air.

I'm not denying the Lord's grace on my life to debate or to take on the critics (with love and truth). And I'm certainly not downplaying the importance of decades of serious study. But I am saying that if I am to make an eternal impact and Jesus is to be truly glorified, it cannot be by human words and human strength alone. The Lord must be anointing and directing and working and intervening. The Spirit must be the operative force in my life. Otherwise, the fruit of my labors will be skin deep.

In the same way, I'm not throwing stones of judgment at my fellow leaders and pastors and preachers and teachers. I'm not saying, "Don't be innovative. Keep the old traditions. By all means, look and sound of out of touch." Not a chance.

But I am saying this. It is all too easy for us to lean on the arm of the flesh, all too easy to measure our effectiveness by the number of our YouTube views, all too easy to be great in the eyes of man and little (or nothing) in the eyes of the Lord.

Paul's Boast vs. Ours

When I write a new book for a publisher, the publicity team (which also prays and seeks to be an effective tool in God's hand) will reach out to me. "How many social media followers do you have? Why should a major media host want you on the air? What is the extent of your reach?"

By God's grace, I can certainly report that we have good numbers, with a substantial social media base, with my articles being reposted all over the internet, and with an endless list of TV and radio appearances on my resume. But does this prove anything? Does this really mean that God is with me? And does any of this mean that even one single soul has been eternally impacted by my life? Absolutely not.

Not only so, but when you compare the fame of our best-known celebrity preachers (by which I mean the Christian leaders best known to the world) to the fame of the biggest worldly celebrities, there is no comparison at all. For every million people who know our names (I say "our" not because I'm a celebrity, but because I'm referring to Christian leaders), there are ten million or 100 million who know the names of the worldly star.

Really now, whoever said that having a million Instagram followers was a sign of divine favor, let alone a sign of anointing, let alone a sign of dedication to God? Hardly! In reality, the biggest Internet stars are often famous for being base, vulgar, and even perverse. Yet how many times have we boasted: "My latest video has gone viral," or, "My latest message is being liked and shared like crazy," or, "My latest book just hit #1 on Amazon in the category of Inspiration."

I've certainly done that, not because I felt this was proof of God's favor, but because I felt it indicated that we had hit a nerve or struck a chord. Yet it is a very small (and subtle) jump from recognizing that people are resonating with our message to believing that the shares or likes or views or sales are a proof of heavenly blessing or divine anointing. Based on that metric, one of the most "blessed" and "anointed" songs of 2020 was a rap song so vulgar and sexually explicit that I cannot quote a line of it here.[3] Based on that same metric, the most "blessed" and "anointed" people on the planet are the Kardashian sisters, especially when they pose in the nude. Can you see, my friend, how misguided we have been?

As one journalist wrote regarding "celebrity" pastors:

> I am not religious, so it is not my place to dictate to Christians what they should and should not believe. Still, if someone has a faith worth following, I feel that their beliefs should make me feel *uncomfortable* for not doing so. If they share 90 percent of my lifestyle and values, then there is nothing especially inspiring about them. Instead of making me want to

become more like them, it looks very much as if they want to become more like *me*.[4]

Here's how Paul "boasted" of his own ministry when he needed to separate himself from the carnal "super-apostles." He wrote:

Are they servants of Christ? (I am out of my mind to talk like this.) I am more. I have worked much harder, been in prison more frequently, been flogged more severely, and been exposed to death again and again. Five times I received from the Jews the forty lashes minus one. Three times I was beaten with rods, once I was pelted with stones, three times I was shipwrecked, I spent a night and a day in the open sea, I have been constantly on the move. I have been in danger from rivers, in danger from bandits, in danger from my fellow Jews, in danger from Gentiles; in danger in the city, in danger in the country, in danger at sea; and in danger from false believers. I have labored and toiled and have often gone without sleep; I have known hunger and thirst and have often gone without food; I have been cold and naked. Besides everything else, I face daily the pressure of my concern for all the churches. Who is weak,

> *and I do not feel weak? Who is led into sin, and
> I do not inwardly burn?*
>
> *If I must boast, I will boast of the things that show
> my weakness. The God and Father of the Lord
> Jesus, who is to be praised forever, knows that I
> am not lying. In Damascus the governor under
> King Aretas had the city of the Damascenes
> guarded in order to arrest me. But I was
> lowered in a basket from a window in the wall
> and slipped through his hands* (2 Corinthians
> 11:23-33).

Somehow, this sounds a little different than a publicist asking me, "Dr. Brown, how many Facebook followers do you have? And on how many radio and TV stations does your broadcast air?" Somehow, this sounds a little different than the way I'm introduced at churches, "Dr. Brown has written more than forty books, preached around the world, and taught at seven leading seminaries." I don't think the Lord is impressed.

Today, being an "apostle" is a sign of prestige, of lofty stature, of being "somebody." Being a senior pastor is really big, but being an apostle is bigger still! Somehow, Paul didn't have that memo when he wrote:

> *For it seems to me that God has put us apostles
> on display at the end of the procession, like*

those condemned to die in the arena. We have been made a spectacle to the whole universe, to angels as well as to human beings. We are fools for Christ, but you are so wise in Christ! We are weak, but you are strong! You are honored, we are dishonored! To this very hour we go hungry and thirsty, we are in rags, we are brutally treated, we are homeless. We work hard with our own hands. When we are cursed, we bless; when we are persecuted, we endure it; when we are slandered, we answer kindly. We have become the scum of the earth, the garbage of the world—right up to this moment (1 Corinthians 4:9-13).

He also wrote this:

We put no stumbling block in anyone's path, so that our ministry will not be discredited. Rather, as servants of God we commend ourselves in every way: in great endurance; in troubles, hardships and distresses; in beatings, imprisonments and riots; in hard work, sleepless nights and hunger; in purity, understanding, patience and kindness; in the Holy Spirit and in sincere love; in truthful speech and in the power of God; with weapons of righteousness in the right hand and in the left; through glory and dishonor, bad report and good report; genuine, yet regarded as impostors; known, yet regarded as unknown; dying, and yet we live on; beaten, and yet not killed; sorrowful, yet always rejoicing; poor, yet making many rich; having nothing, and yet possessing everything (2 Corinthians 6:3-10).

I doubt that Paul would be impressed with many of our big, contemporary leaders. Yet writing from a prison cell, he has made more of a lasting impact on the world than the "biggest" ministries on the planet today. Beware the seduction of success. Beware the snare of outward growth. I urge you to build what will last, not just into the next generation but into eternity. Do not get your eyes on numbers.

Where Is Our Focus?

To say it once more: There are fine mega-churches and large, anointed media ministries. We should use all the tools we have at our disposal, especially the internet. Financial provision is a great blessing, something for which we should be thankful, and numbers can be a real sign of divine favor. My constant prayer is to make the maximum impact on the maximum number of people, all for the glory of God.

But, as we have emphasized, all that glitters is not gold, and there is a very dangerous—even deadly—foreign mixture that has invaded many of our churches and ministries today. It even dominates them.

Go to the latest leadership conference and see if there is an emphasis on prayer, on holiness, on the power of the Spirit, on burden for the lost, on world missions. Or is the emphasis on how to grow a successful church? Or how to market your ministry? Or how to construct a sermon? Or how to manage your budget? Or how to use social media?

These things can have a place, because being practical is important too. The Book of Proverbs is quite practical, isn't it? But it is our dependence on earthly things and our lack of dependence on heavenly things that is our undoing. The greatest proof of this is simple—we desperately need a divine visitation, yet we don't even know it. "We're doing just fine without You, Lord!"

Of course, in our charismatic circles, we go to the other extreme. Our conferences are often marked by themes like: how to have an angelic encounter; or, understanding the mysteries of the third heaven; or, seven new prophetic revelations; or, trance evangelism. (OK. I exaggerated just a bit with the last one.) And all the while, in the midst of our packed-out events, we have people bound by porn, marriages falling apart, believers struggling with depression, and teens on the verge of suicide. Yet the message of repentance is not sounded, sin is not dealt with, and the deepest needs of the attendees go largely unmet.

Consequently, in our charismatic circles, it's not so much that we don't recognize our need for visitation. It's that we think we *are* experiencing an ongoing visitation. "The Shekinah glory is here," we exclaim, "and angels are handing out new anointings as I speak! Who needs revival?"

We have even substituted good music and talented musicians and singers for Christ-exalting lyrics and God-filled worship leaders. As expressed by David Wilkerson in 2002 (for more on this message, see the next chapter):

> I look at the whole religious scene today and all I see are the inventions of ministries of man and flesh. It's mostly powerless. It has no impact on the world. And I see more of the world coming into the church and impacting the church rather than the church impacting the world. I see the music taking over the house of God. I see entertainment taking over the house of God...an obsession with entertainment in God's house, a hatred of correction,

and a hatred of reproof. Nobody wants to hear it anymore.[5]

What makes this Wilkerson quote so powerful is that he appreciated good music, and Times Square Church in New York City, which he pastored for many years, had some excellent musicians and singers. And everything was done at the highest quality with real excellence. Yet in the scores of times I preached there from 1991 to 1995, there was always a deep sense of reverence, there was fervent prayer before the services started, and there was a sense of real dependence on the Lord. And when I would stand to preach, I would do so in the awe of God. I knew I was standing on sacred ground.

I personally love music, coming to faith as a rock drummer in 1971 and having written a whole book on *The Power of Music*.[6] For the last five decades, some of the most joy-filled encounters I have had with the Lord have been during times of singing upbeat praise songs, while some of the most tearful encounters I have had with Him have come while singing soul-stirring songs of worship. In many ways, there is no more powerful tool on the earth than the tool of music.

Yet it is so easy to prostitute our musical talents, to lean on our musical excellence, to so package each song with intros and solos and complex melodies that our gatherings feel more like concerts than worship services and our worship leaders look more like performers than servants. Is this not a very real trap? And with meetings programmed to the minute for the sake of our satellite church broadcasts, have we not also programmed out the moving of the Spirit?

I fully understand the constraints of multiple services where you have to exit the building at a certain time in order to empty the parking lot and clear the seats, lest you end up with a massive traffic jam blocking your community's roads. I understand how the meetings must be coordinated between worship and announcements and preaching and altar ministry, coupled with children's services and the like. And I applaud the workers and leaders who give themselves tirelessly to serve their flocks, often doing five worship sets in a weekend, preaching five sermons, ministering to group after group of children. This is certainly kingdom work, and when I preach in those settings, I nail the timing to the second, trying to sync the final "Amen" with the final zero on the clock. (After all, I'm a radio guy.)

But where, pray tell, is there room for the Spirit to break in? Where does He have control of our agenda? Where can He visit and speak and act, even if it means singing one less song or shortening (or even eliminating) a sermon?

There are churches that have leadership gatherings on Monday to evaluate their Sunday services, and I believe they do this with good motivation, wanting to honor God and serve people. And so they ask: How did the songs flow? Were the vocals too loud? Was the worship team color-coordinated? What about the lighting? And did the pastor's jokes enhance the message? What about his movie illustration? Was that powerful?

Yet all the while, the Spirit is asking His own set of questions: How much time did you spend seeking Me? How much room was there for My ministry? How did the songs exalt Jesus? How did the preaching magnify the cross? Where was the sacred encounter? Where was the dependence on My anointing and power rather than your talent and effort?

Perhaps His questions are more important than ours? Perhaps it's time we review our priorities? And even if time constraints or building constraints make it difficult for us to have prolonged services (after all, if your services run five to six hours, it will be difficult to have three of them on Sunday), why can't we build a culture of prayer that puts secret intercession ahead of public meetings? And why can't we have encounter services on a regular basis where the Spirit can flow freely? And what is stopping us from cultivating a presence-driven mentality in our home meetings?

Let me say once more than I know of mega-churches that emphasize prayer and that really depend on the Lord during their set times of worship. I know of pastors with large followings who really give themselves to intercession and seek God earnestly for their messages. And it is God who is giving them the increase.

I simply ask if we have often substituted the arm of the flesh for the power of the Spirit and if we have mistaken earthly success for the blessing of God. Surely this hits home for many of us, both with large and small ministries. Surely this is always a human temptation, especially in our push-button, digital age.

The Politicizing of the Church

But there is something else that has entered the house of God in recent years, and it is a destructive plague that could totally derail us. I'm talking about cloaking the gospel in an American flag. I'm talking about equating patriotism with the kingdom of God. I'm talking about prophets being moved by a partisan political spirit more than by the Holy Spirit. I'm talking about evangelical and charismatic believers becoming better known for support of a political leader than for loyalty to Jesus. I'm talking about more prayer for the elections than for revival and more concern for getting our candidates in office than for getting our neighbors saved. This has made us into a laughingstock before the watching world, and sadly, we are often the last ones to know it.

I personally voted for Donald Trump in 2016 and 2020, having real reservations about his character and recognizing the damage he could do as our national leader but strongly preferring his policies to those of his Democratic opponents and recognizing the very real threats posed by the radical left. And, looking back in the summer of 2021, I deeply appreciate the stands he took and the courage he showed. In many ways, we are indebted to him.

At the same time, I asked in 2018 if our relationship with him as evangelicals was a match made in heaven or a marriage made with hell, while in 2020 I wrote a whole book asking whether we had passed the Trump test.[7] (What I meant by the "Trump test" was: 1) can we vote for Trump without tarnishing our witness? And 2) can we unite around Jesus even if we divide over Trump?) I can now say that the answer to that question is a categorical "no." We failed that test miserably.

I asked one of my evangelical colleagues, a lifelong Republican but a strong Never Trumper, to articulate his concerns about our relationship with Trump. (I warn you that these words are very strong. If the shoe fits, take them to heart. If they don't apply to you, then don't be offended.) He wrote (in part):

> The evangelical world has made a similar deal with Donald Trump, who is operating in the same manner as Satan did with Jesus [in the wilderness during the Lord's time of temptation]. He is offering the evangelical world what they want... Israel... Abortion... Economy... but at an unacceptable price. The evangelical world has fallen down to worship Trump, not as God, but as the means toward "good things" they seek and admire. In the process, they ignore his ungodliness, cruelty, manipulations, and lying. They made the living God into Donald Trump's back up man. This is foul idolatry. And I mean this utterly.

> The price they have paid for these "good things" they've gotten? The credibility of the gospel and of its messengers. Who can respect a gospel peddled by people who have sold themselves and their integrity so cheaply and hitched their wagon to such an evil, narcissistic man? In a real sense, Trump evangelicals made a deal with the devil. And everybody loses.[8]

Another concerned believer wrote:

> ...it is deeply troubling that Mr. Trump's evangelical supporters refuse to condemn the president's unethical behavior in office. That failure stands in sharp contrast to their reaction to Bill Clinton's moral failings, boldly summed up in a 1998 Southern Baptist resolution. "We implore our government leaders to live by the highest standards of morality both in their private actions and in their public duties," it read, "and thereby serve as models of moral excellence and character."
>
> This sentiment appears all but forgotten when it comes to measuring the current president.

He continued:

> It is a sure sign of a church's internal decay when the sum and substance of its religious activity becomes entwined with political partisanship, especially when loyalty to a political figure is equated with loyalty to God.
>
> At that January Evangelicals for Trump rally [in 2020], the opening prayer included these words: "We declare that no weapon formed against him will be able to prosper and every demonic altar erected against him will be torn

down" and that "he will rise high, and he is seated in the heavenly places."

Christians have traditionally denounced such talk as idolatry.

In this light, it is no wonder that Trump-supporting evangelicals don't comprehend the moral gravity of the lies and contempt that characterize Mr. Trump's words, and that they excuse the manifold corruptions of his office. He's a political messiah, after all; by definition, he can't do wrong.[9]

Again, I know some of the wording sounds harsh or even extreme, especially as Trump fought for our religious liberties, stood for the unborn, appointed solid judges to our courts, helped many poor people with his policies, moved the embassy to Jerusalem and brokered new Middle East peace deals, and faced down Iranian terrorism and the tyrannical rule of China. That's why he got my vote and my support. But I also said this, over and over again: Jesus is my Savior and Lord. He died for me and has my heart and my life and my soul and my all. Trump is my president and he gets my vote. Let there be no confusion between the two!

Sadly, as the media grew more hostile to Trump, as Big Tech censored him and other conservatives, as the left became more radical still, many of us looked to Trump as our champion, the only man who could save America and the free world, God's anointed especially raised up at such a time as this, the man appointed by heaven to fight for our cause. To question him was to question the Lord. To raise any criticism against him was to fail to heed the prophets. To differ with his narrative was to be spiritually disloyal. And, months after Joe Biden was inaugurated as president in January 2021, many prophets were still promising that Trump would soon be back, that Biden was about to be removed, that God was making a list of those who believed their words, ready to punish those who would dare to doubt them. One of the prophets even claimed to have a vision of Trump seated on a throne, ruling from heaven!

This is a real form of idolatry. This is stealing the glory that belongs only to the Lord and giving it to a courageous but very flawed man. Worse still, some of our leaders became the poster boys for Trump, turning a blind eye to his reckless words and making excuses for his destructive behavior. We who once became famous for shouting, "Character counts! Morality matters! We are the Values Voters!" now said, "I can live with Trump's nastiness. He's saving the unborn. I can put up with his lies. He's fighting global terror."

And the world looked on with scorn. We brought reproach to Jesus' name! How desperately we need a sweeping repentance movement, beginning with many of our leaders, beginning with many of our social media influencers, beginning with those of us to whom much has been given. Much will also be required!

Enough with our celebrity Christianity and our superstar spirituality and our partisan political preaching. As the Lord said through Jeremiah, "Stand at the crossroads and look; ask for the ancient paths, ask where the good way is, and walk in it, and you will find rest for your souls" (Jer. 6:16).

Back then, the people responded defiantly, saying, "We will not walk in it." Today I hear a fresh cry, as God's people cry out, "Here we are, Lord, chasing after You! By Your mercy, we are returning to the ancient paths, to the good ways. Our ways have left us cold and dry."

Notes

1. Michael Brown, Twitter @DrMichaelLBrown, December 1, 2020, https://twitter.com/DrMichaelLBrown/status/1333987623321399298.
2. Brown, *It's Time to Rock the Boat*, 287.
3. See Michael Brown, "The Soon-to-Be No. 1 Song Underscores Why We Need a Moral and Cultural Revolution," The Stream, August 13, 2020, https://

stream.org/the-soon-to-be-no-1-song-underscores-why
-we-need-a-moral-and-cultural-revolution.

4. Ben Sixsmith, "The sad irony of celebrity pastors," December
6, 2020, https://spectator.us/sad-irony-celebrity-pastors
-carl-lentz-hillsong/?fbclid=IwAR1a3CxZtvxhgM
cB_eTM4E7Ll8_BijAbRb2oeMWZd44bZ1k37C
-lRRpVi_E.

5. Wilkerson, "A Call to Anguish," https://www.sermonindex
.net/modules/articles/index.php?view=article
&aid=32622.

6. Michael L. Brown, *The Power of Music: God's Call to
Change the World One Song at a Time* (Lake Mary, FL:
Charisma House, 2019).

7. Michael L. Brown, *Evangelicals at the Crossroads: Will We
Pass the Trump Test?* (Concord, NC: Equal Time Books,
2020).

8. Private Facebook message, quoted with permission.

9. Mark Galli, in Ronald J. Sider, *The Spiritual Danger of
Donald Trump: 30 Evangelical Christians on Justice, Truth,
and Moral Integrity* (Eugene, Oregon: Cascade Books,
2000), 7-8. Note that elsewhere I have taken issue with
some of Galli's comments; here, however, I strongly agree.
See Michael Brown, "A Response to *Christianity Today's*
Call for the Removal of Trump from Office," December
20, 2019, https://stream.org/a-response-to-christianity
-todays-call-for-the-removal-of-trump -from-office.

CHAPTER TEN

ASKING THE QUESTION AGAIN: IS IT TOO LATE FOR AMERICA?

In 1989, I wrote my first book on revival, *The End of the American Gospel Enterprise*, with a foreword by Leonard Ravenhill. Chapter Fourteen of the book asked the question, "Is It Too Late for America?" The chapter began with these words:

> Is God through with America? Is He ready to spew us out of His mouth? Is it too late for revival? Is our country ready to die?
>
> Absolutely not! We have definite proof that He is beginning to move. *He is judging the house of God.* He is bringing us down before

He lifts us up and "smiting" before He heals. *Revival could be at the door.*

Sometimes great revival precedes great judgment, and other times great judgment precedes great revival. *Revival and judgment go hand in hand.* We stand somewhere in that cycle today.

Four years later, in 1993, when we released a repaginated version of the book, I made a slight adjustment here, changing the words from "Absolutely not!" to "Maybe not!"[1]

I believe this was prompted in part by my association with David Wilkerson at that time, as I was preaching for him regularly at Times Square Church and hearing more of his message of impending judgment. It might also have been the result of further reflection on prophetic language in the Bible, as in Joel 2, where the prophet calls for deep repentance and then states, "Who knows? He may turn and relent and leave behind a blessing" (Joel 2:14).

He didn't leave the people hopeless, nor did he assure them that all would be well. The former could produce despair, leading to depression and inaction. "It's too late, and there's nothing you can do!" The latter could produce complacency, leading to a false optimism and, again, to inaction. "Don't worry! God is merciful and will forgive."

Instead, Joel struck a holy balance, calling his people to a place of absolute dependency on the Lord: "It could be too late, but I truly hope it is not. Appeal to the Lord while there is still time!"

His words were urgent and compelling. Without God's mercy, it was all over. With His mercy, there was still hope. It is with a similar sense of urgency that I write these words more than three decades after the publication of *The End of the American Gospel Enterprise*.

I truly believe that we could be in the very early stages of a powerful spiritual outpouring, one that could sweep America from coast to coast. And I truly believe that, as impossible as it seems, America's greatest days could be ahead. A massive awakening could leave massive changes in its wake. All things are possible with the Lord.

But I also understand that America as we know it could soon be gone forever, that we are teetering on the edge of a steep precipice, and that we could quickly pass the point of no return. Can you sense that urgency too? Is it almost too late for our nation?

In 1985, David Wilkerson released the book *Set the Trumpet to Thy Mouth* using words taken from Hosea 8:1, words also reflected in the title to Chapter Seven of this book. In this incendiary little volume, Wilkerson spoke of the grievous sins of America and predicted that, very soon, the whole nation would explode—literally, vanish—the result of a hydrogen bomb. In the opening lines of the book, he wrote:

> "Behold, the name of the Lord cometh from far, burning with his anger, and the burden thereof is heavy: his lips are full of indignation, and his tongue as a devouring fire. And the Lord shall cause his glorious voice to be heard, and shall shew the lighting down of his arm, with the indignation of his anger, and with the flame of a devouring fire, with scattering, and tempest, and hailstones" (Isaiah 30:27,30). "Yea, the stork in the heaven knoweth her appointed times; and the turtle and the crane and the swallow observe the time of their coming; but my people know not the judgment of the Lord" (Jeremiah 8:7).
>
> America is going to be destroyed by fire! Sudden destruction is coming and few will escape. Unexpectedly, and in one hour, a hydrogen holocaust will engulf America—and this nation will be no more.

Why this fiery judgment? Wilkerson explained:

It is because America has sinned against the greatest light. Other nations are just as sinful, but none are as flooded with gospel light as ours. God is going to judge America for its violence, its crimes, its backslidings, its murdering of millions of babies, its flaunting of homosexuality and sadomasochism, its corruption, its drunkenness and drug abuse, its form of godliness without power, its lukewarmness toward Christ, its rampant divorce and adultery, its lewd pornography, its child molestations, its cheatings, its robbings, its dirty movies, and its occult practices.

In one hour it will all be over. To the natural mind it is insanity to come against a prosperous, powerful nation and cry out, "It's all over! Judgment is at the door! Our days are numbered!" The church is asleep, the congregations are at ease, and the shepherds slumber. How they will scoff and laugh at this message. Theologians will reject it because they can't fit it into their doctrine. The pillow prophets of peace and prosperity will publicly denounce it.

But Wilkerson was not concerned about what people had to say, as he wrote:

I no longer care. God has made my face like flint and put steel in my backbone. I am blowing the Lord's trumpet with all my might. Let the whole world and all the church call me crazy, but I must blow the trumpet and awaken God's people. Believe it or not, America is about to be shaken and set aside by swift and horrible judgments. Many other praying believers who have been shut in with God are hearing the very same message—"Judgment is at the door! Prepare, awaken!"[2]

These are stirring, shocking, devastating words. How should we respond to them?

Hanging by a Thread of God's Mercy

On the one hand, given the gravity of our nation's sin and the degree of light to which we have been exposed, any judgment we receive would be merited. We hang by a thread of God's mercy. On the other hand, would God use a nuclear holocaust to wipe out hundreds of millions of people, including tens of millions of believers, because of the sins of the nation?

When it comes to our national guilt, there is no limit to the depth of our depravity, even if abortion was the only major sin of this nation. (Sadly, we are guilty of many other grave sins.) Just imagine what it would look like if the bodies of more than sixty million slaughtered babies were piled on top of each other as a witness against America. Would anyone question the Lord's right to destroy us on the spot?

Still, the Lord has never spoken to me about a coming fiery judgment on our nation, so I cannot say "yea" or "nay" to David Wilkerson's prophecy. But I can say that, in many ways, he spoke as a prophet to our country, calling out the evil deeds of the world and speaking to the compromised state of the Church. And remember: he wrote this in 1985, long before we descended as deeply into our current cultural and moral morass. What would he say if he were alive today? (Brother Dave, as we called him, died in a car accident in 2011 at the age of 80.) How much more urgent would his message be?

You might say, "It's obvious he wasn't speaking by the Spirit, because his words of imminent judgment never came to pass and he said it would happen very soon."

That is true, although, oftentimes, our "very soon" is quite different from God's "very soon," and a prophet might sense the Lord's judgment at the door when it is decades and decades away. But what if the Lord *has* judged us, only in a different way? What if His judgment was *not* to intervene with a massive explosion, one which would have destroyed the righteous with the wicked? What if His judgment was simply to let us go our own way? What if He chose not to stop us from sinning by blowing us off the map but rather judged us by giving us over to our sins? What if the great judgment was to allow us to reap what we have sown? That is a terrifying prospect.

Perhaps just this one image from 2017 in Long Beach, California is enough to turn our stomachs. It is a picture of a drag queen with satanic horns, reading to babies and toddlers in a library, with the blessing and approval of the parents. Imagine it in your mind, or click on this link to see it for yourself.[3] Where are we headed next? Where might we end up in ten or twenty more years? Who would dare imagine?

We all know the inspired account in Romans 1, where Paul said this of the human race:

> *For although they knew God, they neither glorified him as God nor gave thanks to him, but their thinking became futile and their foolish hearts were darkened. Although they claimed to be wise, they became fools and exchanged the glory of the immortal God for images made to look like a mortal human being and birds and animals and reptiles.*

Therefore God gave them over in the sinful desires of their hearts to sexual impurity for the degrading of their bodies with one another. They exchanged the truth about God for a lie, and worshiped and served created things rather than the Creator—who is forever praised. Amen.

Because of this, God gave them over to shameful lusts. Even their women exchanged natural sexual relations for unnatural ones. In the same way the men also abandoned natural relations with women and were inflamed with lust for one another. Men committed shameful acts with other men, and received in themselves the due penalty for their error.

Furthermore, just as they did not think it worthwhile to retain the knowledge of God, so God gave them over to a depraved mind, so that they do what ought not to be done. They have become filled with every kind of wickedness, evil, greed and depravity. They are full of envy, murder, strife, deceit and malice. They are gossips, slanderers, God-haters, insolent, arrogant and boastful; they invent ways of doing evil; they disobey their parents; they have no understanding, no fidelity, no love, no mercy. Although they know God's righteous decree that

> *those who do such things deserve death, they not only continue to do these very things but also approve of those who practice them* (Romans 1:21-32).

Does this foretell the fate of America? Will we continue to degenerate until we self-destruct? That remains a very real possibility.

And yet, the final verdict has not been issued and the last word of this current chapter has not been written. We could also be on the verge of the greatest awakening in American history. Perhaps out of the chaos and pain and division and anarchy of 2020, a powerful revival will arise. Perhaps the deep darkness will give way to glorious light. Why not?

Yet we must not let this very real hope produce an attitude of complacency. God forbid. I cannot relate to such a mindset, especially at such a critical time in our history.

And Yet...

Since my earliest preaching as an 18-year-old in 1973, I have been bringing a message of repentance, confronting the evil of our generation. And many a time, I have laid on my face in the presence of God, shaking—I mean that literally—in light of the greatness of His holiness and the grossness of our sin.

That's why *The End of the American Gospel Enterprise* in 1989 was followed by *How Saved Are We?* in 1990 and *Whatever Happened to the Power of God?* in 1991. That's why, in more recent years, some of my books have included *Outlasting the Gay Revolution* (2015), *Saving a Sick America* (2017), *Jezebel's War with America* (2019), and *Revolution: An Urgent Call for a Holy Uprising* (2020, this is the second, revised edition of my 2000 book). I *do* understand the urgency of the hour and the gravity of our situation. And yet...

In his book *Renaissance: The Power of the Gospel However Dark the Times*, respected Christian thinker Os Guinness reminds us of the power of God's "and yet," writing this about the life of Jesus:

> What were the odds that a rural carpenter's son from an obscure backwater of the Roman Empire would outshine the pride and glory of the greatest emperor and the mightiest warrior captains of history? How likely was it that the birthday of a man viewed as a disgraced and executed provincial criminal would come to mark the year that for most of the world divides all history? As Christopher Dawson noted, from the perspective of a secular historian the life of Jesus "was not only unimportant, but actually invisible."

And yet. And yet.[4]

He also writes this:

> So yes, we strive for excellence. We know that nothing less than our best is worthy of our Lord. Our concern is always to achieve our utmost for his highest. We know that leaders have more influence than followers, that the center of a culture has an influence that far outweighs the periphery, that kings outweigh commoners, that the rich can get far more done than the poor, and that the well-educated know far more than the average person.
>
> We know all that, we respect all that, and we take it seriously—and yet, and yet. So we are also always ready for the surprising voice, the far-from-obvious leader, the last-person-you-would-ever-think would be the key player. And yes, we are always ready to recognize God's nobodies and God's fools. For these may be the truly anointed ones prepared to be seen and treated as nobodies and fools for Christ's sake, whom God uses far more than we who are the obvious ones for God to use.[5]

Could this be the perfect time for a massive divine surprise?

The thing that gives me the greatest hope is that God has put a cry in the hearts of His people. Believers across the nation have been seeking Him earnestly for a fresh outpouring, a tendency I began to notice more markedly in the second half of 2019. Then, the crisis of 2020—meaning that the whole year was a crisis—caused that cry to go deeper. And, I repeat, it was God Himself who put the cry in our hearts and moved us to pray. Why would He do this if it was too late for America? Why would He move us to pray if He didn't intend to answer our prayers? Why would He raise our vision for revival and build our faith for awakening if He only planned judgment and destruction?

Matthew Henry once said, "When God intends great mercy for His people, the first thing He does is set them a-praying." I ask you, then: Would God have set us to praying if He had no intention of showing mercy? And could there be such sustained intercession for revival if the Lord did not initiate it?

That being said, the clock is definitely ticking, and unless the intensity of our cry meets the intensity of the hour, we might well miss this divine window of opportunity. And so, as I ask the question again, "Is it too late for America?" I hear the Spirit saying, "You tell Me."

The Lord is saying that the answer to that question is up to us.

In other words, if we will humble ourselves and repent, if we will seek Him as if our lives depended on it, if we will pray like Jacob and say, "I won't let you go until You bless me," if we will give ourselves unconditionally to the work of the gospel, then the answer could well be "Absolutely not! It is not too late for America." But if we become complacent, if we put our trust in numbers, if we treat God's mercy lightly, if we do not seek Him with desperation, if we somehow believe that we can make it without a holy visitation, then the answer could well be, "I gave you time to repent, but you did not."

Right now, even as more and more prayer ascends to heaven for our nation and for revival, there is still a real sense in which we are praying to preserve our American lifestyle rather than praying because we are jealous for the glory of God and because the fate of the nation depends on it.

The truth is that the Church of America is in a precarious place, the nation hangs in the balance, and yet the Lord is ready to move.

What, then, will it be?

Notes

1. Michael L. Brown, *The End of the American Gospel Enterprise* (repaginated printing; Shippensburg, PA: Destiny Image, 1993), 81.
2. Wilkerson, *Set to the Trumpet to Thy Mouth*, 1-2.
3. See https://losangeles.cbslocal.com/2017/10/16/draq -queen-library-lgtbq-kids.
4. Os Guinness, *Renaissance: The Power of the Gospel However Dark the Times* (Downers Grove, IL: InterVarsity Press, 2014), 64.
5. Ibid., 107.

CHAPTER ELEVEN

From Revival to Awakening

Every week during the Brownsville Revival, I would say to the many new visitors in our services, "You can no more schedule a revival than you schedule an earthquake. You can no more hold a revival than you can hold a hurricane. Revival is not something that man works up. Revival is something that God sends down."

I said those words because, in some parts of America, especially our southern states, "revival" refers to a series of special meetings, something you put on your calendar once a year, an event that you "hold." That's why I would constantly say that we cannot "hold" or "schedule" a revival. Simply stated, if we can schedule it and produce it, it is not a revival.

But how, exactly, should we define revival? This is the definition I developed while teaching our students at the Brownsville Revival School of Ministry: "Revival is a season of unusual divine visitation resulting in deep repentance, supernatural renewal, and sweeping reformation in the Church, along with the radical conversion of sinners in the world, often producing moral, social, and even economic change in the local or national communities."

The beginning of this definition gives the essence of revival—it is a season of unusual divine visitation. The end of the definition explains how revival in the Church can lead to awakening in the society—it often produces moral, social, and even economic change in the local or national communities.

Charles Finney put it like this: "[A revival] presupposes that the Church is sunk down in a backslidden state, and a revival consists in the return of the Church from her backslidings, and in the conversion of sinners."[1] A true revival will always touch the world.

And so, with the Church revived (which means loving Jesus passionately, walking in sacrificial love, living in holiness, preaching the gospel in power), and with sinners being saved (which is the direct result of a reinvigorated Church and the real presence of the Spirit), awakening can follow. This is the only hope of our nation and the only way to reverse our moral and cultural decline.

The flames of fire ignited by revival bring light to the whole nation. The transformation of individual lives leads to the transformation of culture. Revival brings spiritual reformation to the Church and cultural revolution to the world. Can you imagine what awakening would look like in America today?

"Are You Ready?"

Three months prior to the Father's Day Outpouring, the Sunday service in 1995 when the revival began in Pensacola, my book *From Holy Laughter to Holy Fire: America on the Edge of Revival* was published.[2] I sensed that something was about to break in America—a repentance-based, Jesus-exalting, revival—and the purpose of the book was to help prepare the way for this coming visitation.

This is how the last chapter of the book ended, a vivid description of what was about to burst on the scene in Pensacola:

> Once, while preaching near Buffalo, I visited Niagara Falls together with Jennifer, our older daughter. As we walked along the bank towards the Falls, there was a clear, strong tide

pulling the waters along. The thought struck me: "That is the state of a growing church. It is progressing and moving forward. But that is not revival."

Then we got nearer to the Falls. The flowing stream had turned into raging rapids! The water was capped with white waves, and the tide was almost violent in its pull. Again the thought came to mind: "That is what most of us today call revival. It's a great increase over the normal state of things, much more is happening, and it looks really exciting. But it's still not revival!"

Then we came to the Falls. They were absolutely awesome! I had seen them as a little boy, but the reality was so much more powerful than the memory. They were not just grand and impressive. They were staggering!

But I wasn't content just to see the Falls. I wanted to experience them. So Jennifer and I joined a group of other interested tourists, rented out some big, yellow rain coats, left our shoes in a locker, and went down to the rocks at the base of the Falls. The closer we got, the more overwhelming it became.

Torrents of water—so much water!—crashed like thunder. In a moment we were soaked. The wind—where did it all come from?—blew so hard it actually took our breath away. We were no longer spectators. We were participants, caught up in the pounding, swirling, churning, flooding display of natural glory. There, in a face to face encounter with the raw power of God, with the majesty of the Creator exploding all around me, I could only raise my hands and praise Him who lives for ever and ever. I was swallowed up in the Falls.

That is a picture of revival. Are you ready?[3]

Roughly ninety days later, torrents of living water were poured out in Pensacola, and the rest is history—a history that is still being written. That's because the story is still unfolding in the lives of the many lost sinners who were saved through the revival, the many backslidden believers who returned to the Lord, the many casual believers who were set on fire, along with the many ministries that were birthed. Also, through the revival's ministry school, a powerful missions movement was birthed, a movement that itself multiplied into several different streams. There is much to the story of the Brownsville Revival still to be told.

One of those missions streams, overseen by our team at FIRE International, has sent out more than 250 family units since the late 1990s, totaling more than 350 people. They have served in more than forty nations, with some of them remaining on the field for more than two decades now. Other grads from our ministry school, also touched by the fires of revival, are powerful evangelists, leading thousands or even millions of people to Jesus. Other grads are raising their children to be world-changers, ready to impact the next generation with the realities of the gospel.

That's why we pray, "Do it again, Lord! But this time, let the revival be even more widespread, even more Jesus-glorifying, even more world-impacting." All things are possible with the Lord.

What Revival Fire Looks Like

Once again, in order to paint a picture of just what our God can do, putting you in remembrance of what we saw Him do in the 1990s, allow me to share what some of those attending the revival had to say. This is not to be nostalgic. Instead, it is to stir your hunger and raise your vision:

> I have been saved 40 years. I have been in the district for 20 years and at this school for

9 years. I have never seen a move of God in schools like what we have since the [Brownsville] Revival began. Kids tell me, "I got saved, my attention deficit is gone, I can study. I've been released from getting up every morning hating my uncle for some abuse that occurred when I was younger. I've been released from drugs." One girl said she used to not want to live, she was controlled by drugs, depressed, and it's all gone.

—Dr. Charles Woolwine
Vice-Principal, Niceville High School,
where hundreds of students were
transformed through the revival[4]

And this:

I have prayed for revival for 51 years, 5 months, and fifteen days. I have led and raised up revival prayer movements through most of these years. At last I have seen it—at Brownsville. I felt like Simeon who saw God's salvation after many years, and then asked if he could depart in peace!! You can see how encouraged I was while with you.

—A letter from Rev. Alex Buchanan, England,
after visiting the Brownsville Revival[5]

And this:

> I must tell you that since attending the [Brownsville leadership] conference in November [1996], my own life has been profoundly affected. I feel like I have been born again all over again (I realise that's what is meant to happen in revival) and am experiencing the presence of God in a way I have never done before. I arrived home with great expectancy but also with no agenda to try and make something happen. The first Sunday I was back, I stood in front of the congregation here in Alton to greet the people and just broke down uncontrollably. Many in the congregation began to do the same.... I did manage to deliver the Word the Lord had given me the night before. I knew I had to, as I was experiencing such a burden in my heart in a way I have never experienced before. I spoke from Isaiah 6..."I have seen the Lord...Woe to me, I am ruined! For I am a man of unclean lips and live among a people of unclean lips and my eyes have seen the King, the Lord Almighty." I gave opportunity to the people to respond and every single person came forward to repent and be cleansed.... There are many things I

could share, but just to say that there is a new spirit over the people. People want to worship and pray in a way they've never done before and have a whole new desire to see their families, friends and neighbours saved.

—E-mail from a British pastor after his visit to the Brownsville Revival[6]

And how did it feel to those of us who were privileged to participate in countless revival services after years of praying and crying out and fasting for this very thing? After a particularly glorious and intense service, even for the revival (it took place Friday night, January 31st, 1997), I returned home at 1:30 in the morning and was moved to write these words:

I want to share my heart honestly with you, holding nothing back. I want to make myself totally vulnerable. The fact is, I *must*.

I have just come from the beautiful presence of the Lord, from a night of glorious baptismal testimonies and incredible stories of wonderfully changed lives, a night of sovereign visitation, a night of deep, sweeping repentance, of radical encounters with the living God, of public acts of repentance—from young people throwing their drugs and needles into the garbage to old people discarding their cigarettes—a night of weeping under conviction and rejoicing in new-found freedom, a night when the Spirit fell upon the children in a side room until their intercession and wailing permeated the sanctuary, a night when Jesus was exalted in the midst of His Church. Yes, I have come from the holy presence of the Lord in the Brownsville Revival on January 31st, 1997. The Spirit moved, the tears flowed, the Lord touched, the demons fled. This is what happens when revival is in the land!

At the end of the night, amidst shouts of joy and victory, amidst the sound of the newly redeemed enjoying their first moments free from captivity, I turned to my dear friend, Evangelist Steve Hill and said, "We don't have to quote from the history books about revival. It's here! We're seeing it before our eyes."

Who can describe a night like this? Who can describe what it is like to be so caught up with God that heaven is virtually here and you can almost sense the sound of the Judge knocking at the door? What can you say when young men come to the platform and begin to throw away their earrings, and another wants counsel because he doesn't know how to remove his *eyebrow* ring, and another tosses out his condoms, while another throws his knife into the trash? What can you say?

What can you say when a thousand people respond to the altar call and stay there for two hours getting right with God? What can you say when the prayers you have prayed for your nation, prayers for the real thing, for genuine visitation, for bona fide outpouring—not hype, not sensationalism, not a superficial show, but an awakening of historic proportions—when those prayers are being answered before your eyes and you know that you know that your country will be *shaken*? What can you say?

What can you say when all you want is Jesus, when pleasing Him is your total delight, when you just have to tell everyone about God's great salvation, when sin's sweetest temptation is utterly repulsive to you, when you just can't find the words to express to the Lord how utterly wonderful He is, how He really is your all in all? What can you say at a sacred time like this? It is too precious to fully describe, too intimate to wholly communicate with mere human speech.[7]

Yet all of this was only a foretaste. There is so much more the Lord wants to do, and there has never been a better time than now.

Why can't amazing light arise in the midst of deep darkness? Why can't the rain of God's Spirit fall on this dry and parched land? Why can't a sustained revival, exploding in communities across the country, lead to a true awakening? Why can't a visitation become a habitation that sweeps our land from coast to coast? Why can't the words of a holy God prick the conscience of a hardened people? Why can't the power of a loving God heal the hearts of the hopeless? Why can't America be known as a country of justice, of righteousness, of compassion, of ethics? Are not all things possible with the Lord?

And isn't *this* the very time that revival is needed most, when so much of the Church is compromised and confused and carnal? Isn't *this* the very hour that awakening must happen, when so much of the society is hostile to God and hardened to the gospel?

Allow me to quote these words to you again, words that were so real when I wrote them in 1997, words which spoke of such incredible potential through the Lord, and words which pointed to a vision still to be fulfilled: "What can you say when the prayers you have prayed for your nation, prayers for the real thing, for genuine visitation, for bona fide outpouring—not hype, not sensationalism, not a superficial show, but an awakening of historic proportions—when those prayers are being answered before your eyes and you know that you know that your country will be *shaken*? What can you say?"

Could it be that this vision is nearer, not further away, than ever? Could it be?

Is Another Great Awakening at the Door?

For several decades now, prayer movements have spread through our nation, including weekly city-wide prayer gatherings; massive, one-day prayer events; and 24-7 harp and bowl prayer (meaning, prayer that is expressed through worship). And through the year 2020, as our nation was devastated by the impeachment hearings, the COVID-19 crisis (including the lockdowns and shutdowns), the deaths of George Floyd and others, leading to protests and riots and chaos, then the hotly contested presidential elections and widespread claims of fraud, fervent prayer was ascending to God from coast to coast.

We were repenting. We were searching our hearts. We were praying for mercy. We were confessing our need. And we were taking the gospel to the streets. Yes, right in the middle of the protests and riots, the gospel was being preached, captives were being set free, and new believers were being baptized in portable tanks.

Could this be a sign of a greater outpouring to come? Could it that God's people, finally getting desperate, have begun to seek Him earnestly? Could this be the hour that a national revival turns into the greatest awakening in our history? Could this be the moment we have dreamed about, prophesied about, prayed for, and preached and proclaimed?

In my 2017 book, *Saving a Sick America*, I wrote this:

> John Zmirak, a conservative Catholic columnist who holds a Ph.D. in English from Louisiana State University, told me that when he was a student at Yale, his professors uniformly praised communism, making clear that it was communism, not capitalism, that was the key to the world's future success. They were quite confident that this socialist system was here to stay, with its sphere of influence growing by the decade. Who would have imagined how dramatically and quickly it would collapse around the globe? And, Zmirak asked, who would have believed that the principal players who would help topple communism would be a former Hollywood actor (Reagan!), a female Prime Minister in England, the daughter of a lay preacher and grocer (Thatcher!), a shipyard

worker who became the head of a Polish trade union (Walesa!) and a Polish pope (John Paul II!).

What does God have planned for America? What unlikely players is He preparing to use? Who can tell how swiftly and dramatically the tide could turn in our land? And if we as His people truly humble ourselves, confessing our sins, recognizing our need, and giving ourselves unconditionally to the Lord, what surprises will He have in store for our nation? Could it be that our greatest awakening is ahead of us rather than behind us?

Things look so bad today that many believers wonder if God can really save our very sick nation. But if He truly is God (and He is!), the answer is simple: All things are possible to him (or her) who believes (see Mark 9:23-24). The question is: Do we really believe? If we really do believe God and His Word, then we will be willing to take holy, Jesus-glorifying, counterculture action based on our faith, regardless of cost or consequence. Forward in faith without flinching!

On April 8, 1966, *Time Magazine* featured a stark front cover (for the first time, without a picture of any kind) simply asking the question in bold text, "Is God Dead?" Five years later, on June 21, 1971, the *Time* cover story featured a picture of a hippie-like Jesus with the caption, "The Jesus Revolution." Who saw this coming?

Even more interesting is the fact that pollsters in the early 1960s predicted that the young generation would be a joy to work with, a generation that really honored authority. Not quite! These pollsters had no clue that a massive counterculture revolution was about to rise, a nation-shaking revolution led almost entirely by young people. And these same pollsters never could have imagined that in the midst of this rebellious movement a sweeping religious revival known as the Jesus Revolution would arise as well. Perhaps another great awakening is right around the corner for us, an awakening as near as it is undetected?[8]

I ask again: Why not?

The question, again, comes down to our hunger, to our desperation, to our desire. How badly do we want to see revival in the Church and awakening in the society? God will not pour out His Spirit where there is not sufficient room to contain it. God will not visit in power where He is not deeply desired. But He *will* pour out water on the thirsty land. He *will* satisfying the longing of our souls. He *will* respond to the cries and tears and repentance of His people. After all, He wants to visit us more than we want to be visited.

So what will it be? Will the pockets of outpouring in 2020 continue to spread? Will we continue to emphasize *being* the Church even more than we emphasize going to church services (which, of course, is important too)? Will we get even hungrier for the Spirit's visitation—more dependent, more desperate, more devoted—refusing to let go until our cities are shaken? Will we refuse to quit until America is ablaze with the fire of revival, leading to a moral and cultural awakening? And then, will we seize the moment and consolidate our gains by being the salt of the earth and the light of the world?

I write these words several months after my sixty-sixth birthday, having walked with the Lord for nearly fifty years, and at this age, although I feel as youthful as a teenager, I have no interest in playing games. Talk is cheap, and I assure you that I've heard it all by now. The big, amazing, incredible prophecies of "the coming move of God" are a dime a dozen.

Like you, I want to see the real thing. To touch it and walk in it again (but even deeper and more widespread this time). I want to see the possibilities of what the Lord can do through yielded vessels. I want to see Jesus so glorified in the eyes of a watching world that the most hardened skeptics and mockers will fall to their knees confessing Him as Lord. And if He doesn't return in my lifetime, I want historians to be able to write about the greatest awakening ever experienced in America, the one that took place in our day.

Does that describe your heart too? Then turn the page and lift up a prayer. Perhaps God has a special plan for you.

Notes

1. Charles G. Finney, *Revival Lectures* (Old Tappan, NJ: Fleming H. Revell, n.d.), posted online at https://www.whatsaiththescripture.com/Text.Only/pdfs/Revival_Lectures_Text.pdf, 5.
2. This was the title of the second edition of the book, reflecting how I initially wanted to title it but was overruled by the first publisher who sadly missed the times and seasons in which we were living.
3. Brown, *From Holy Laughter to Holy Fire*, 265-266.
4. Quoted with permission in Brown, *Revival Answer Book*, 84.
5. Quoted with permission in ibid.
6. Quoted with permission in ibid., 84-85.

7. Ibid., 40-42. You can watch parts of that actual service here: https://www.youtube.com/watch?v=-jyntPNKLlc.
8. Brown, *Saving a Sick America*, 184-185.

CHAPTER TWELVE

THE WORLD HAS YET TO SEE

"The world has yet to see what God can do with a man fully consecrated to him." These were the words made famous by the great evangelist D.L. Moody, but the quote did not originate with him. It's true that he added his personal Amen, saying, "By God's help, I aim to be that man." Yet the actual quote originally came from Henry Varley, a British revivalist whom Moody met in Dublin, Ireland.

It was Varley who made the comment to Moody in 1872, just before Moody returned to America. The quote changed Moody's life. But one year later, Varley didn't remember saying those specific words. For him, it was just a passing comment. Yet it was a comment that rocked Moody's world.

As recounted by Varley in 1873:

During the afternoon of the day of conference Mr. Moody asked me to join him in the vestry of the Baptist Church. We were alone, and he recalled the night's meeting at Willow Park and our converse the following morning.

"Do you remember your words?" he said.

I replied, "I well remember our interview, but I do not recall any special utterance."

"Don't you remember saying, 'Moody, the world has yet to see what God will do with a man fully consecrated to him?'"

"Not the actual sentence," I replied.

"Ah," said Mr. Moody, "those were the words sent to my soul, through you, from the Living God. As I crossed the wide Atlantic, the boards of the deck of the vessel were engraved with them, and when I reached Chicago, the very paving stones seemed marked with 'Moody, the world has yet to see what God will do with a man fully consecrated to him.' Under the power of those words I have come back to England, and I felt that I must not let more time pass until I let you know how God had used your words to my inmost soul."[1]

Oh, what a calling! What an invitation! "The world has yet to see what God will do with a man (or woman) fully consecrated to him." What is stopping you? What is stopping me?

I can honestly say that, to a certain extent, I have done my best to live my life without regrets, to leave it all in the ring, as they say in boxing. I have done my best to go for it, to run my race so as to win, to make my life count, to redeem the time. I don't want to look back at the end of my days here on earth and say, "If only! I only I had really gone for it. If only I had really lived for God. If only!"

Yet, in another sense, I know that I have *not* fully done this. Absolutely, categorically not. Not a chance. Not even close. I have not truly found out, over a consistent period of years, what would really happen if I sought God as if nothing else mattered, if I believed every divine promise as if it were really true, if I genuinely lived every hour in the light of eternity, if I really went for it, if I fully consecrated myself spirit, soul, and body. I cannot afford to live the rest of my life without finding out!

What about you? Do Varley's words speak to you as well? Do they challenge you the way they challenged Moody? Do they light a fire in your own soul? Do you hear yourself crying out, "Then let me be that one!"?

What would happen if you shut out every distraction and sought the Lord with all your heart and all your soul? What would you happen if you said "no" to everything unnecessary and unessential, spending every free hour on your face before God crying out for breakthroughs, for visitation, for transformation, for empowerment? What would happen if you did this for one week, let alone for weeks or months on end?

What would happen if you stepped out in deeper faith, putting greater emphasis on obedience than on playing it safe? What would happen if you gave the Lord more of your heart, allowing Him to share His burden with you more deeply until His pain became your pain and you participated in His travail? What would happen if you pursued holiness as if your life depended on it, asking the Lord to conform you to the image of His Son Jesus? What would happen?

I've seen the Lord do amazing things through my life and ministry over the decades, all to His glory and for His honor. And I have often sought Him passionately. As I mentioned earlier, when I was saved for about one year, it was my daily habit to spend six or seven hours alone in the Word and prayer. And I did that for about six months without missing a day, until a full-time job, and then college, made that schedule impossible. (I also did my best to share the gospel with at least one new person every day.)

I've had periods of years when I consistently cried out for revival fire to fall and for the glory of God to flood my soul, fasting and praying with earnestness and passion. And I've gone for it in terms of ministry activity, preaching and teaching and traveling and writing and pouring my soul out for others with schedules that would exhaust most people.

Yet I know there is a deeper place. A deeper place of singlemindedness. Of consecration. Of intimacy. Of love. Of service. Of holiness. Of encounter. In fact, I know there is a *much deeper place*.

And I sometimes wonder, "How many more people could I touch, for the glory of Jesus' name, if I just slowed down and spent more time before the Lord? How much deeper and lasting would the impact be? What would my life and ministry look like if I gave myself over to the Lord in an all-consuming, total way and sought Him as if my very life depended on it? If only!"

Do you resonate with these words? Is your heart crying out even as you read? If so, what is stopping you from taking the plunge?

The Ministry of John G. Lake

I first discovered the ministry of John G. Lake (1870–1935) around 1983 when I started teaching at Christ for the Nations Biblical Institute in Stonybrook, New York. (This was a branch of the famous Christ for the Nations Institute based in Dallas, Texas.) As I read some of his sermons, one of them, called "Spiritual Hunger," jumped out to me.[2] In the words of Lake, "No matter what your soul may be coveting, if it becomes the supreme cry of your life, not the secondary matter, or the third or fourth, the fifth, or tenth, but the supreme desire of your soul, the paramount issue—all the powers and energies of your spirit, soul and body are reaching out and crying to God for the answer—it is going to come!"[3]

What a calling to holy desperation, to seek the fullness of the Spirit, to long for the Lord and desire Him and go after Him until He touches you in the innermost part of your being. Yes, God fills the hungry! God satisfies the thirsty![4]

My precious wife Nancy often shared with me another quote from Lake, and even as I see the words again now, they sting my heart afresh: "Beloved, for the sake of a dying, suffering world, count the cost, pay the price, get God's power, and set the captives free." How can we say no?

To be clear, this is not a matter of earning something from God, of torturing our bodies to twist His arm, of fasting and praying and sacrificing enough until we somehow attain the heavenly blessing. Instead, it is a matter of holy partnership, of sacred co-working, of putting ourselves in a place of intense commitment and complete sacrifice so that we belong wholly to Him, so that He can consume us with His grace and anointing and wisdom and power, so that we are so absorbed in Him and so yielded to Him that He can trust us with more of His very presence. What's stopping you? What's stopping me?

What Lake was talking about was a condition of the heart more than anything else. It is a desire that can burn in us while we work our jobs and take care of the responsibilities of life. It is a hunger and a cry that is unquenchable. It is a passionate longing that is undeniable.

I have experienced this many times over the years. I have groaned and travailed in intercession. I have sought to give God every fiber of my being and determined to follow Him whatever the cost or consequence. But I have also let up. I have also gotten busy, especially doing the work of ministry. And, relatively speaking, I have gotten comfortable, at least in part. Oh, for that holy fire to burn with full intensity once again!

Just think about the apostle Paul, one of the true heroes of the faith. No matter how deeply he knew and experienced the Lord, he wanted to go deeper. He wanted to be used more. Speaking of his earlier life as a religious Jew with a great spiritual pedigree, he wrote:

I once thought these things were valuable, but now I consider them worthless because of what Christ has done. Yes, everything else is worthless when compared with the infinite value of knowing Christ Jesus my Lord. For his sake I have discarded everything else, counting it all as garbage, so that I could gain Christ and become one with him. I no longer count on my own righteousness through obeying the law; rather, I become righteous through faith in Christ. For God's way of making us right with himself depends on faith. I want to know Christ and experience the mighty power that raised him from the dead. I want to suffer with him, sharing in his death, so that one way or another I will experience the resurrection from the dead!

I don't mean to say that I have already achieved these things or that I have already reached perfection. But I press on to possess that perfection for which Christ Jesus first possessed me. No, dear brothers and sisters, I have not achieved it, but I focus on this one thing: Forgetting the past and looking forward to what

*lies ahead, I press on to reach the end of the race
and receive the heavenly prize for which God,
through Christ Jesus, is calling us* (Philippians
3:7-14 NLT).

That is how Paul lived his life: "with hands out-
stretched to whatever lies ahead," going "straight for
the goal" (PNT). He was reaching forward with all the
divine energy inside of him. His eyes were on the prize.
He was so consumed with a vision of Jesus that he going
to be that man—that man of whom Varley spoke. The
world has certainly seen what God could do through a
yielded vessel like Paul. The reverberations are being felt
to this moment.

Lake also said this: "One of these days we will get
sick and tired of the spiritual bankruptcy that we live in
and the joke that our lives often are and we will get serious with God!"

Perhaps the whole reason I wrote this book was so
that you—yes, you—could read these words and say,
"Lord, I'm ready to get serious! Start Your work in me!
And let the world see who Jesus really is—through me."

Maybe This Is Your Story Too

Let's go back to the amazing Hebrides Revival (1949–
1952), one of the greatest examples of a sovereign move

of God in history. People were saved so dramatically during that revival that altar calls were not even given, and it was estimated that the vast majority of those who came to faith did so outside of church buildings, often in fields or bars or dance houses. Duncan Campbell shares the amazing origins of this incredible work of the Spirit—and note carefully that one of the things that most prompted intercession for revival was that young people had dropped out of church. Does this sound familiar in our day?

Campbell tells the story, starting at the beginning.

> Now I am sure that you will be interested to know how, in November 1949, this gracious movement began on the island of Lewis. Two old women, one of them 84 years of age and the other 82—one of them stone blind— were greatly burdened because of the appalling state of their own parish. It was true that not a single young person attended public worship. Not a single young man or young woman went to the church. They spent their day perhaps reading or walking but the church was left out of the picture. And those two women were greatly concerned and they made it a special matter of prayer.

A verse gripped them: "I will pour water on him that is thirsty and floods upon the dry ground." They were so burdened that both of them decided to spend so much time in prayer twice a week. On Tuesday they got on their knees at 10 o'clock in the evening and remained on their knees until 3 or 4 o'clock in the morning—two old women in a very humble cottage.

Do you see that? It was two old women, one totally blind and other bent over with arthritis, who helped pray in this mighty outpouring. Perhaps this speaks to one of you reading this book right now—maybe in your sickness or old age or confinement? Perhaps your prayers could change the course of history? Perhaps Henry Varley's words are sparking a holy challenge in *you* right now?

The story continues:

One night, one of the sisters had a vision. Now remember, in revival, God works in wonderful ways. A vision came to one of them, and in the vision she saw the church of her fathers crowded with young people. Packed to the doors, and a strange minister standing in the pulpit. And she was so impressed by the vision that she sent for the parish minister. And of

REVIVAL OR WE DIE

course he knowing the two sisters, knowing that they were two women who knew God in a wonderful way, he responded to their invitation and called at the cottage.

That morning, one of the sisters said to the minister, "You must do something about it. And I would suggest that you call your office bearers together and that you spend with us at least two nights in prayer in the week. Tuesday and Friday if you gather your elders together, you can meet in a barn-a farming community, you can meet in a barn-and as you pray there, we will pray here." Well, that was what happened, the minister called his office bearers together and seven of them met in a barn to pray on Tuesday and on Friday. And the two old women got on their knees and prayed with them.

And now we come to a key part of this account, a very sacred moment. And note carefully who is used by God to break things open: a "young man, a deacon in his church"—not an elder, not a famous leader, not some Christian superstar. Just a young servant.

Well that [prayer] continued for some weeks—indeed, I believe almost a month and a half. Until one night—now this is what I am anxious for you to get a hold of—one night they were kneeling there in the barn, pleading this promise, "I will pour water on him that is thirsty, floods upon the dry ground" when one young man, a deacon in the church, got up and read Psalm 24. "Who shall ascend the hill of God? Who shall stand in His holy place? He that has clean hands and a pure heart who has not lifted up his soul unto vanity or sworn deceitfully. He shall receive the blessing (not a blessing, but the blessing) of the Lord."

And then that young man closed his Bible. And looking down at the minister and the other office bearers, he said this—maybe crude words, but perhaps not so crude in our Gaelic language—he said, "It seems to me to be so much humbug to be praying as we are praying, to be waiting as we are waiting, if we ourselves are not rightly related to God."

And then he lifted his two hands—and I'm telling you just as the minister told me it happened—he lifted his two hands and prayed, "God, are my hands clean? Is my heart pure?" But he got no further. That young man fell to his knees and then fell into a trance. Now don't ask me to explain this because I can't. He fell into a trance and is now lying on the floor of the barn. And in the words of the minister, at that moment, he and his other office bearers were gripped by the conviction that a God-sent revival must ever be related to holiness, must ever be related to Godliness. Are my hands clean? Is my heart pure? The man that God will trust with revival—that was the conviction.

And that was the spark. That was the word (and prayer) that ignited the revival.

When that happened in the barn, the power of God swept into the parish. And an awareness of God gripped the community such as hadn't been known for over 100 years. An awareness of God—that's revival, that's revival. And on the following day, the looms were silent, little work was done on the farms as men and women gave themselves to thinking on eternal things gripped by eternal realities.[5]

Within days, meetings were being held in church building after church building until the early hours of the morning, and a "strange minister," someone from the outside, Duncan Campbell, was being used to preach and lead. He walked into a sovereign move of the Spirit, a bona fide, heaven-sent revival, and he was as stunned as any to see what God was doing.

And to what human instrumentality does he credit these amazing results? Whom did Campbell say helped usher in this visitation, and who were the principle players who kept the flames alive? The two elderly sisters; a small army of prayer warriors, including farmers and postmen and blacksmiths and busy mothers and local pastors; young people dramatically saved from their carnality, suddenly called to preach the gospel; children gripped by the holy presence of a holy God; former alcoholics now living sober lives.

They were, in the sight of man, a bunch of nobodies. But in reality, who else does God have to use? Who else does He choose to use? As Paul wrote:

> *But God chose the foolish things of the world to shame the wise; God chose the weak things of the world to shame the strong. God chose the lowly things of this world and the despised things— and the things that are not—to nullify the things that are, so that no one may boast before him. It is because of him that you are in Christ Jesus, who has become for us wisdom from God—that is, our righteousness, holiness and redemption. Therefore, as it is written: "Let the one who*

boasts boast in the Lord" (1 Corinthians 1:27-31).

Isn't now the perfect time to cry out to the Lord, "Then surely You can use me, Lord!" Isn't now the perfect time to consecrate your life to Him afresh? Isn't now the perfect time to take the first step—and then the second and the third—to find out just what God could do through you? Isn't now the perfect time to put the past behind you—including all its failures and disappointments, which all of us have—and to say, "Lord, let today be a brand new day!"

And to all of those with "big" ministries and large churches and masses of social media followers and abundant financial resources, the words of James Gilmore (1843–1891), who served sacrificially as a missionary to Mongolia, speak to us afresh:

> Do we not rest in our day too much on the arm of flesh? Cannot the same wonders be done now as of old? Do not the eyes of the Lord run to and fro throughout the whole earth, still to show Himself strong on behalf of those who put their trust in Him? Oh, that God would give me more practical faith in Him! Where is now the Lord God of Elijah? *He is waiting for Elijah to call on Him.*[6]

So call on Him today. And then call on Him tomorrow, and the next day, and the next, until the fire of God has taken hold of your life and your heart and your mind and your soul. Let the revival start with you and with me! It is revival or we die.

Notes

1. Cited in Mark Fackler, "The World Has Yet to See...," Christianity Today, https://www.christianitytoday.com/history/issues/issue-25/world-has-yet-to-see.html.
2. John G. Lake, *Spiritual Hunger and Other Sermons* (ed. by Gordon Lindsay; Dallas, TX: Christ for the Nations, n.d.), 5-18.
3. Ibid., 7.
4. See Psalm 107:9; John 7:37-39; Revelation 22:17.
5. Duncan Campbell, "Revival in the Hebrides," The Revival Library, http://www.revival-library.org/index.php/pensketches-menu/historical-revivals/the-hebrides-revival.
6. James Gilmore, *James Gilmour of Mongolia: His diaries, letters, and reports by James Gilmour* (Project Gutenberg, March 6, 2010), Journal Entry for September 11, 1870, https://www.gutenberg.org/ebooks/31525.

About Michael L. Brown

Dr. Michael L. Brown holds a Ph.D. in Near Eastern Languages and Literatures from New York University and has served as a visiting or adjunct professor at seven top seminaries. The author of more than thirty books, he hosts the *Line of Fire* radio program, a syndicated, daily talk show, where he serves as "your voice of moral, cultural, and spiritual revolution," and his syndicated columns appear on many Christian and conservative websites. He is considered to be the leading Messianic Jewish apologist and has been engaged in Jewish dialogue and outreach for more than 45 years. Michael and his wife, Nancy, have two children and four grandchildren. They live near Charlotte, NC.